# Trust the Timing
## A Memoir of Finding Love Again

By JoAnne Macco

Copyright © 2017 by JoAnne Macco

All rights reserved.

ISBN: 0998602116

All rights reserved.
No part of this book may be reproduced by any means, nor transmitted, nor translated into a machine language without the written permission of the author.

## Author's Note

*Trust the Timing* is written primarily from two points of view. I am thankful beyond words for the patience of those I interviewed to gather details from their memories to add to my own. Some dialogue was recreated from memory, though some is remembered verbatim. There are no composite characters in this book, though some names, identifying characteristics, and locations have been changed to protect privacy.

# Contents

Prologue (2011) .................................................. 1

1. First Love .................................................... 3
   (1971–1972) – JoAnne
2. Learn to Adapt ............................................. 14
   (1960–1972) – David
3. The Moving Gremlin ..................................... 31
   (1961–1972) – JoAnne
4. Moving On .................................................. 47
   (1972–1973) – David
5. Save the Whales! .......................................... 55
   (1972–1977) – JoAnne
6. Fast Cars and Close Calls ............................... 74
   (1973–1976) – David
7. It's So Easy to Fall in Love ............................. 83
   (1977–1989) – JoAnne
8. New Responsibilities ................................... 105
   (1975–1995) – David
9. The Days Are Long, but the
   Years Are Short .......................................... 125
   (1989–1999) – JoAnne
10. Just Work Harder! ...................................... 133
    (1995–2005) – David
11. Ms. Responsible ........................................ 141
    (1999–2000) – JoAnne
12. NO MORE ................................................ 150
    (2005–2009) – David
13. Grief Can Make You Blind ........................... 159
    (2001–2006) – JoAnne

14. **Know Who Your Friends Are** ...................... 183
    (2009) – David
15. **Walk by Faith** .............................................. 192
    (2006) – JoAnne
16. **Awakening** .................................................. 200
    (2009–2010) – David
17. **Finding "Me" Again: Midlife Adventures** .... 213
    (2006–2007) – JoAnne
18. **Believe in Your Dreams** ............................... 225
    (January–May 2011) – David
19. **Family, Friends, and Forgiving** .................... 233
    (2008–2010) – JoAnne
20. **You Never Know What You Might Find** ....... 242
    (June 2011) – David
21. **The Power of Letting Go** ............................. 248
    (January–June 2011) – JoAnne
22. **Reunion** ...................................................... 257
    (July 2011) – David
23. **Cloud Nine** .................................................. 267
    (July 2011) – JoAnne
24. **Home and Back Again** ................................ 273
    (July–October 2011) – David
25. **It's Never Too Late** ..................................... 279
    (July–October 2011) – JoAnne
26. **Birthday Weekend** ...................................... 291
    (October–December 2011) – David

**Epilogue (2012)** ................................................. 300

This is for all the lonely people.

# Prologue
## (2011)

On the Tuesday night after my daughter's high school graduation, I sat down at the computer in the hallway alcove. It had been another long day at work with more computer time than I'd ever imagined possible for a counseling job. My hands ached and my eyes wanted to close as I scanned the inbox for important emails, then diverted to Facebook, hoping to relax. A private message was waiting for me.

I clicked the icon and stared at the name for several seconds as my weariness evaporated. Warmth spread through me like a mild hot flash, and my heart pounded as I read the message:

Greetings to you!
After many years,
I hope you are well.
Take care and be safe!

I looked at the name again, then sat back from the computer.

Could it really be him? My first love, from back in the seventies?

I took a deep breath. So much had happened since then. College, career, two kids, twenty years of marriage,

## Trust the Timing

and the unexpected divorce that rocked my foundation and ripped my self–esteem to shreds.

It had taken years to regain my footing. I'd sewn myself back together, one piece at a time. Loose threads of self-doubt showed up less often now. Sleeping alone finally felt normal. I'd come to appreciate the extra space, though I didn't mind the dogs sleeping with me in the winter. Unlike my ex, the dogs hardly ever snored. My most loyal companions, the dogs provided more comfort and less stress than the men I dated after the divorce. So for the last five years I'd remained single and celibate, reciting the words I'd seen on a T-shirt:

It's better to have loved and lost,

than to live the rest of your life with a psychotic.

Cultivating cynicism about romance helped me feel safe. When loneliness tugged at my sleeve, I pushed it away. Guarding my serenity was more important, and I couldn't afford to let my sanity be compromised again. The stress of unhealthy relationships had probably taken a few years off my life already, and I hoped to live long enough to enjoy a few golden years, even if it turned out to be just me and my dogs. I had almost given up on romance.

And now, this simple message on Facebook, from the high school sweetheart I hadn't heard from in almost forty years, stirred up memories from another lifetime.

I closed my eyes and smiled as my mind drifted back to the fall of 1971.

# 1

## *JoAnne*

# First Love
(1971–1972)

October's cool air brought relief from the summer heat and added excitement to the new school year. As I walked the three blocks to Terry's house, newly fallen leaves danced in the street, urging me to pick up my pace. It was Saturday, and I was going to hang out with my best friend. We sat on the floor in her pastel bedroom with the paper flowers and peace posters and listened to Melanie and Carole King until we got bored and started to lament about not having boyfriends. Then Terry's eyes lit up.

"I know! Let's have a party!"

"You mean a Halloween party?"

"No. That's for kids. I'm talking about a *cool* party. Maybe my parents will let us have it in the garage."

This would be nothing like our usual Saturday-night sleepovers. No *Tonight Show* with Johnny Carson. No Chef Boyardee pizza in a box. No prank phone calls. It would be our first real high-school party with boys, and possibilities swirled around in my head like the autumn leaves.

# Trust the Timing

In two months, I would be sixteen and still had not had a decent first kiss. That awkward moment in the backyard with Harold from down the street laying on top of me didn't count. His impatient kiss bruised my lips with urgent pressure. It lacked imagination and certainly didn't get him any further.

Caroline, our friend with the big, beautiful lips, described kisses that sounded like the exact opposite of Harold's, like the luxurious, delicious kiss that lasted the entire length of the song "Crystal Blue Persuasion." I wondered if I would ever have a kiss like that.

"I'm not even sure *how* to French kiss," I admitted.

"Oh, don't worry about it," Caroline encouraged. "Just let it happen naturally."

"That's easy for you to say," Terry argued. "I still can't forget Tommy Rayburn putting his bubble gum in my mouth when he kissed me. It was disgusting! I had more fun kissing my bedroom mirror."

Before the party, Terry and I plastered one wall of her parents' garage with psychedelic black-light posters across from her Bob Dylan poster on the other side. Along with Dylan, we played Black Sabbath and Led Zeppelin. A friend brought over a flashing strobe light with the warning that it could make some people feel sick if you left it on too long, so we used it sparingly.

As people arrived through the kitchen and started mingling, Terry and I looked at each other and grinned. This was going to be good. Her parents hardly checked

## A Memoir of Finding Love Again

on us but greeted people at the front door and directed them to the garage. We were pretty well-behaved anyway. If anything bad happened, it happened in the back seat of somebody's car, though few of us had cars back then.

I felt a wave of shyness as the room started to fill up and went to sit on the large trunk at the back of the garage. Terry, however, floated from person to person, welcoming everyone and laughing. I was satisfied to sit back and take in the scene.

In walked this tall, lean guy who grabbed my attention right away. He must have been at least six feet tall. At five foot eight, I was still awkwardly taller than most guys my age. He looked a lot older than someone in tenth grade, like he could easily pass for a senior. He wore an olive-green military field jacket over a T-shirt and jeans. His wavy blond hair fell over his eyebrows but didn't cover his ears. He smiled slightly as someone caught his attention. Caroline waved at him from across the room with a big smile, and he walked over to her. I realized he must be the one she invited from her French class.

I surveyed the room, thinking maybe I should try to mingle. But it was so much easier to just watch. I looked back at the tall guy standing with Caroline and a couple of other people. It wasn't just his height that attracted me. There was something about him, a look of maturity in his soft eyes as he listened, not saying much. His focus drifted from the conversation, and he caught me

# Trust the Timing

staring at him. The 7UP bubbles dancing in my paper cup suddenly became very interesting.

From my perch, I watched out of the corner of my eye as he walked to the cooler to get a soda. When the strobe light came back on, I lost sight of him as more people came in.

"Turn that damn thing off!" somebody yelled a few minutes later.

When the regular lights came back on, I started to scan the room and almost jumped when he appeared on my right, standing next to the trunk, like he'd always been there.

"I guess somebody doesn't like the strobe light," he said.

"Yeah, it's kinda weird," I said, recovering. "But it's cool to watch people moving in slow motion."

"A lot of people here," he said, looking around at the crowd as I sipped my drink.

"Do you know Caroline?" I asked.

"Yeah, she's in my French class."

"I take French too. Third period. It's one of my favorite classes." I wondered how dumb that sounded.

"Je m'appelle David." He smiled gently and gave a slight bow.

"Un *bon* nom," I said. I'd always liked the name David. I don't know why. It just felt like a strong name. "Je m'appelle JoAnne."

"Do you mind if I join you?" he asked, motioning to the trunk.

## A Memoir of Finding Love Again

"No, I don't mind," I managed to say and scooted over to make room.

We practiced our French (still just talking, not kissing) and made small talk about school.

"You don't have a Southern accent," David observed.

"That's because I moved around a lot. My dad was in the Marines."

"My father was in the Navy *and* the Army. That's why I can't let my hair cover my ears." On cue, he tilted his head to tuck any stray hair behind one ear.

"It's a good thing I was born a girl, or I'd probably have a crew cut," I empathized.

"I'm glad you're a girl too." He smiled. "I like your hair like it is." He held my gaze for an extra second and looked like he wanted to touch my hair, but he didn't. My heart beat faster as Carole King sang "I Feel the Earth Move."

For as long as I could remember, I'd felt different with my wavy red hair and freckles. Mom used to say my hair was strawberry blonde, trying to soften taunts of, "There goes the redheaded woodpecker." She told me movie stars paid good money for curls like mine. But I didn't start to appreciate my hair until I was in my thirties. At fifteen, getting a compliment on my hair from someone my own age, especially a good-looking guy, felt like a dream.

As we sat together that night in Terry's garage, David listened to me thoughtfully, his bluish-gray eyes watching

## Trust the Timing

my face or my hands, not roving around the room. I felt like he cared about what I said. Instinctively, I felt safe with him.

At school on Monday, I kept a lookout for David and spotted him in between classes. He stood near the doorway of the building I was headed for. Was he looking for me? He smiled when he saw me.

"I had a good time talking with you at Terry's party," he said.

"Yeah, me too. I had a good time too." I didn't know what else to say.

"Hey, is it okay if I call you?" he asked.

"Sure. Um, you want my number?"

"That would be nice." He pulled out a pencil, looked at me with his attentive blue eyes, and said, "Ready."

I told him my number and he wrote it in his notebook. Then we both hurried off to class. After school, I found out Terry and Caroline had given him tips on my schedule so he'd know where to find me. Caroline was fine with me being interested in him, even though she had invited him to the party. What a great friend!

David called me that night and asked if I'd like to go to a movie with him. We didn't talk long. Later, he explained that his father only allowed him to be on the phone for three minutes at a time. I wondered about that but didn't pry.

On our first date, David's mom dropped us off at the movies. She was really nice and looked like Sophia

## A Memoir of Finding Love Again

Loren, though she was Scottish, not Italian. The movie, *Billy Jack*, was about a quiet hero who defended American Indian kids and his girlfriend's hippie school from the local bad guys.

During a sad part in the movie, David took my hand and held it gently in his. I leaned in a bit closer and felt the warmth of his body as my heart beat faster. After a few minutes, he reached to put his arm around me. I felt protected by David's closeness as I watched Billy Jack fight off the bad guys who way outnumbered him. Then, during a slow scene, I turned to look at David in the soft light. He moved his face closer, and his lips touched mine. I closed my eyes and was glad I was sitting down so I wouldn't faint. Our first kiss was more than decent. It was magical. Gentle, yet with a hint of passion that would grow with practice. It lasted at least a minute, during which I had no idea what happened in the movie or that I was even in a movie theater. I managed to refocus on the movie before its emotional ending and theme song, "One Tin Soldier," that I would remember forever.

After the movie, we walked across the street for pizza and talked about *Billy Jack*—the racial injustice, Billy Jack's motorcycle, and wouldn't it be cool to go to a school like the one in the movie where you get to learn about whatever you're interested in? David held my hand as we walked back to the movie theater , where his mom picked us up and drove me home. He walked me to the house and gave me a kiss on the cheek. I floated up the front steps.

# Trust the Timing

Over the next few weeks, I got to know David better. His favorite band was Jethro Tull because their music was different, not mainstream. He'd often hum "Aqualung" or "Wind Up" very quietly, so you almost couldn't hear him. He worked on motorcycles and did odd jobs at his uncle's shop. I thought it was cool that he knew how to fix things like my dad. He had a nice smile and a quiet sense of humor. He was always considerate, never pushy.

In early December, David gave me a ring for my birthday. It was a guy's ring his mother had given him for his birthday, but since he didn't like to wear jewelry, he wanted me to have it. The ring was gold with a dark-blue stone and way too big for me, but I loved it. I wrapped blue yarn around it so it would fit and wore it for the rest of the school year as a symbol that I had a steady boyfriend. But David wasn't just a boyfriend. He was my first love. At sixteen, I couldn't imagine feeling that kind of love for anyone else.

There was an underlying sensitivity about David. Sometimes he got quiet, and a look of frustration or sadness came upon him for no apparent reason. One Saturday afternoon, I met him at the motorcycle shop to wait for him to get off work so we could go to the movies. He focused on putting a motorcycle together, as I sat on the cement floor of the garage and watched. He had on his work jeans with the battery-acid holes.

"Would you hand me that wrench?" he asked.

"Which one is it?"

## A Memoir of Finding Love Again

I was good at academics but a bit embarrassed not to know about practical tools.

David smiled kindly. "I shouldn't expect you to know that," he said and reached for it himself.

After he finished the job, we walked to the movie theater. David seemed preoccupied, like he was going over a conversation in his head.

"Is something wrong?" I asked.

"No, it's nothing . . . just some stuff going on at home."

Then he took my hand and smiled at me with his eyes.

"This is gonna be a weird movie, you know," he said, changing the subject. We were going to see *Harold and Maude*. "It's about an older woman and a younger man."

"You mean like us?" I grinned. David was eleven months younger than me.

"No. A way older woman. Eighty or something."

"Hmmm." I was intrigued. "Well, I heard it's got Cat Stevens music, so it's gotta be good."

David nodded and hummed a Jethro Tull tune as we got in line to buy tickets.

I wondered briefly what might be going on at home that he didn't want to talk about. I didn't know much about David's father, but his mother was friendly and kind. She got frustrated at times, having her hands full with three adolescent boys. But she was always very nice to me, like the time she let me put eyeshadow on her while we waited in the car for the boys to finish at the motocross track. And she was great about driving us around.

On Fridays, David walked home from school with me, and his mom picked him up later. On weekends, we walked to the DQ or the movies, or we hung out with Terry and Caroline in the neighborhood. When Caroline got her license, she was nice enough to chauffeur us in her little beige Falcon to the drive-in to see *Play Misty for Me*. Caroline sat up front to watch the movie and to give us some privacy. David and I sat in the back seat and didn't see much of the movie.

We did a lot of kissing. We kissed in my backyard and at school in between classes and after football games when David came to meet me near the bleachers. I had to sit with the drill team next to the band in my cardinal-red drill team outfit and white go-go boots with red pom-poms.

David's soft, slow kisses made me feel all tingly and treasured. But as amazing as those kisses were, we were smart enough to not let things go too far. We promised each other we wouldn't go all the way until we were sure we were ready. David, at fifteen, was already responsible and a gentleman. It was wonderful to be so in love, to be cherished and respected.

Not that it was easy to abstain from sex with all the hormones soaring in and around us, but our moms helped. When we hung out at each other's houses and made our way to the bedroom, our moms diligently

## A Memoir of Finding Love Again

reminded us to "Open that bedroom door! And keep it open!" They reminded us over and over again. It was annoying to be interrupted, but we sensed our moms were just doing their jobs.

It was an early spring day when David walked me home from school in the middle of the week. His jaw looked tense as his eyes focused on the road ahead. When I asked him if something was wrong, he changed the subject.

We got to my house and went to the backyard where my dog, Lobo, grabbed a tennis ball and brought it to David as usual. David had always liked playing with Lobo. But today, he tossed the ball like it was a sack of potatoes.

"What's wrong?" I asked.

He took a deep breath. "I have some bad news. We're moving. My family's going back to Connecticut . . ."

The details were lost in a shock wave. Then I heard something about "as soon as school's out."

"What? You're *moving?*"

# 2
## *David*
# Learn to Adapt
(1960–1972)

It had been quite a culture shock moving to North Carolina in 1971. And I was just starting to feel comfortable when I found out we were moving back to Connecticut. I didn't want to leave, but at fifteen, what choice did I have?

At least Connecticut was familiar. I'd lived there since the age of four, when my father was assigned to the base in New London. When I was five, we moved to a town so small the locals referred to it as Hooterville, after the town in the sixties TV show *Petticoat Junction*. But in this small town, we had a lot more room than in the cramped military apartments my brothers and I were used to as Navy brats. Here we had a three-bedroom house, our own yard, and trees to climb! We grew up outside most of the time, playing baseball in the summer and sledding and ice-skating in the winter. In the summers, I mowed lawns and went fishing at a nearby pond. In the winters, I shoveled snow. Life seemed normal on the surface.

I was always a little confused about my father. When

## A Memoir of Finding Love Again

you grow up seeing your friends with a mother and a father who are both around all the time, you sort of get the idea that's what it's supposed to be like. But in some ways, it was okay that my father was gone a lot because I never knew what kind of mood he'd be in. One day he was nice and full of laughter; the next day he'd be in such a rage there was nothing I could do to justify my breathing air. I tried to keep my distance. But sometimes, there was no avoiding him.

Every Saturday morning when my father was home, I got my head shaved. Then I had to stand at attention in the backyard and get screamed at (or worse) for some menial chore that I had not done properly. This ritual started by 7:30 a.m. and was a regular part of my week when I was five and six years old. By the time I was seven, my father wasn't home as much, so the routine wasn't consistent. But not knowing when he'd be home, I felt scared out of my mind half the time.

When he was in a good mood, he called me by my name. Other times he called me "boy" or "stupid boy."

"Get over here, *boy*" filled me with dread. "Now look what you've done, *stupid boy*" was demoralizing. I felt like I couldn't win.

On "normal" days, Mom had orders to be up and dressed by 5:00 a.m., with makeup on and no curlers in her hair, to cook his breakfast of bacon, eggs, toast, and home fries. On Christmas Day, the traditional holiday argument broke out by 10:00 a.m. and resulted in my

## Trust the Timing

father leaving the house and not coming back until late in the evening. Every year, I'd wait for the fight to start. When he left the house, I could breathe normally.

My father's behavior was much better when Mom's parents were around on holidays or weekends. Grampa Malcolm was my father figure. If it had not been for him, I would have grown up to be a very different person. It took many years for me to appreciate the depth of his wisdom.

Though he lacked a formal education, Grampa was a genius with tools or anything mechanical. After the hurricane of 1938, he rigged an old car to pump water for Plainfield, Connecticut, for several days. You could tell he enjoyed his work as a machinist by the way he talked about precision. He took pride in making parts and tools to order, beyond the tolerance specification of a thousandth of an inch his customers requested. He milled pieces to fit perfectly within ten thousandths of an inch, so they would last longer.

When the kids got too loud, Grampa retreated down to his basement workshop, which was forbidden to us as children for safety reasons. When he started to run a machine, the lights in the rest of the house dimmed, and we'd hear humming and whirring with an occasional thump. If we peered down from the top of the stairs, we could see the silhouettes of machines, but we weren't allowed to go beyond the top step and never thought of challenging this boundary of Grampa's sanctuary.

## A Memoir of Finding Love Again

Grampa was not fond of church. His mother was Catholic and his father Protestant, so both churches looked down on the whole family because of the "mixed marriage." As a child, my mother was afflicted with undulant fever from drinking unpasteurized milk. The local pastor came by, and toward the end of the visit told my grandfather to pray for a painless death.

Upset with the preacher's lack of hope, Grampa decided he'd had enough of organized religion. "If you can't preach something better than that, then get out of my house!" he declared. Grampa worked out with weights every day, stood six foot one, weighed over two hundred pounds—and he was mad.

The pastor nodded and made a hasty retreat.

My grandparents gave my mother an early Christmas that year, just in case, but she fully recovered under their loving care.

Like Grampa, Grandma Edna didn't care for organized religion. As a child growing up in a crowded foster home, she'd been forced to memorize scripture passages and to recite the books of the Bible forward and backward. In those days, foster children were used mainly for house labor, and Grandma felt like the Bible lessons were a form of regimentation to keep them in line. Grandma had a kind heart, but she didn't take any nonsense and wouldn't tolerate hypocrisy. She did not think too highly of my father, and I'm told that back in the late 1950s, she almost threw a beer can at him.

## Trust the Timing

Mom told me the beer can story many years later. It started with Mom going shopping with her sister Nancy, who was studying to be a nurse. The fact that Aunt Nancy lived with other women fueled various forms of criticism from my father, implying that she only liked women. My father had dropped us off at Mom's parents' while he went to spend time with his friends at the VFW. I stayed with Grandma and Grampa while Mom and Aunt Nancy went downtown and met up with their friend, Tony, who was also studying to be a nurse. They brought Tony back to their parents' house for a nice visit, and he left shortly after my father got there to pick us up. Mom said that after Tony left, my father needled her relentlessly, making fun of her male friend who wanted to be a nurse. Grandma didn't say anything, but she shot daggers at my father with her eyes as his sarcastic remarks continued. As my father got in the car to leave, Grandma grabbed a beer can and drew back her arm to throw it at him, but her arm froze above her head. She told Mom later that God, who she'd claimed she didn't believe in, must have grabbed hold of her arm and stopped it. I can hardly remember a time that we visited my grandparents when my father went in to visit with us.

When I was eleven, my father transferred from the Navy to the Army to enhance his retirement benefits and obtained a commission as a warrant officer assigned to Fort Eustis, Virginia. A one-year tour in Vietnam was part of the deal, and my mother decided we would stay in Connecticut. As the antiwar movement gained momentum, service people and their families were not treated well. We went to a store one day where peace activists walked along the sidewalk, carrying signs. They talked to Mom about stopping the war in Vietnam.

"My husband is serving in Vietnam," she said. "I want him home safely."

"DEATH TO THE WAR PIGS!" they yelled.

"Not in front of my kids!" Mom snapped, and kept us moving.

She didn't tell me until years later about the hate mail she got from pacifists. She shielded us from most of the turmoil, so we lived mostly normal lives. During that year, our home was peaceful with just Mom, me, and my two younger brothers.

On my father's return stateside, he had a few weeks of leave before going back to Virginia to finish his tour of duty. We stayed in Connecticut. Mom talked about him coming home and his retirement from the Army.

"Then we'll all be a family again," she said with a faraway look. She must have been hoping for a long time that my father becoming a civilian would fulfill her dream of a traditional family settled happily in her home state. I don't know if he told her that would happen, or if it was just a dream of hers. I wondered if that kind of family was even possible for us.

At first, he came home once a month, then every

## Trust the Timing

couple of months. Thanksgiving and Christmas of 1970 came and went without my father. I sort of got used to him not being there. Sometimes, at the end of the month, Mom asked me if I had any money to help her with groceries. I'd lend her a twenty from my yard-work or snow-shoveling earnings until her allotment check came in the mail.

In spite of the financial challenges, having family and friends close by made life simple and good. In our tiny New England town, everyone knew everyone else, so it was safe. If we did challenge authority and screw up, we heard about it when we got home because somebody had made a phone call. We knew what to expect.

Then one afternoon, in January of 1971, we had a surprise visit from my father's younger brother, Uncle Ted, whom I'd never met. My father's family was a bit of a mystery. We were told our paternal grandfather died from a heart attack during the height of the Great Depression, when my father was eleven. I'd only seen my father's mother once, when I was twelve and my father was in Vietnam. My uncle from New York took me, Mom, and my brothers to visit my father's mother who lived about two hours away. She seemed happy to see us but wasn't feeling well, so we didn't stay long. Years later, I found out that when my mother wrote to my father that we'd gone to see his mother, he wrote back that she was never to go there again. To this day, I don't know why a man would forbid his wife and children from visiting his mother. It must have been something painful.

I'd heard I had a rich uncle who lived in North Carolina. When I got home from school that day in January, the man was sitting at the kitchen table talking with Mom.

"This is David," Mom told him.

He stood up and shook my hand. He was a little shorter than me. "It's nice to meet you," he said with an air of friendly confidence.

"This is your Uncle Ted," Mom said. "We're having a conversation, so you need to go somewhere."

I went down to the basement to watch TV. About forty-five minutes later, Mom called down that Uncle Ted was getting ready to go. We shook hands again before he left.

"Why was Uncle Ted here?" I asked Mom.

"He was in the area and just stopped by to say hello."

A few days after the strange visit, Mom informed us she was flying to Virginia to see our father. Grandma and Aunt Nancy watched over us. Before we knew it, the weekend was over, and Mom was back.

"There's been a change in plans. We're moving," she announced upon her return.

"Where to?"

"To Virginia to be with your father until he gets out of the Army. Then we're all moving to North Carolina, and your father's going to work with your Uncle Ted."

Moving was a huge shock for all of us. I didn't

## Trust the Timing

understand the urgency to move in the middle of the school year. At fourteen, I was just getting established in high school. I thought we were fine just being the four of us.

In the span of a few weeks, the house sold, and we were on the road on a Friday afternoon in February. Mom drove through the night as I navigated, letting her know when a turn was coming up. We got to Virginia around five in the morning.

It was a tense and confusing three months in Newport News. The five of us lived in a two-bedroom town house while we finished the school year and my father's tour of duty. Most of our neighbors were also military people in transition, and all my friends were in Connecticut.

It was 1971, and with busing mandated by the federal government, I was assigned to a different high school from most of the neighborhood kids. The school I went to was a brand-new cement palace with a cement courtyard that was being finished up by prisoners in chains chipping away at the overpoured concrete. At lunch, I'd ask the prisoners how they were doing, and we made small talk as the armed guards watched.

"You see that man over there?" an older prisoner said. "If I do anything stupid, he'll shoot me." I guess he was trying to influence my thinking, which he did. That was not a life I wanted to lead.

While living in Virginia, we'd drive to North Carolina every few weeks. My parents looked for a place to live, and we hung around with our newfound cousins. On Memorial Day weekend, we headed to Jacksonville and our new house. There was a growing element of excitement for this move. We were getting to know our new relatives, so having family there already would ease the transition.

That summer, I worked for my uncle, uncrating and setting up motorcycles and pumping gasoline. On the off hours, my cousins and I headed to the beach or rode dirt bikes. We could use the racetrack for free during the week when there were no races. Riding motorcycles was a blast. When a bunch of us practiced, we'd end up racing each other. Competition challenged us to go faster and faster and to try new things, like sliding through corners around the oval track. I learned to use my inside foot as a pivot, feathering the power to maintain speed and control. Then, coming out of the apex of the turn, I'd get back into the throttle and feel the tire bite and launch me like a rocket! It was my first real foray into the exhilaration of adrenaline.

At the start of the school year, I was part of the sophomore class and meeting new people. On Fridays, I went to football games and still worked part time at the motorcycle shop or the racetrack when I could for some cash. The move was turning out okay.

One day at school, Caroline, from my French class, invited me to a party at Terry's house. I knew Terry from my history class. I accepted the invitation and thought

## Trust the Timing

this was pretty cool. It would be my first real party. Over the years, I'd passed on a lot of opportunities requiring parental permission because I didn't know how my father would react. But I decided it was time to take a chance. To my surprise, he said yes. I must have caught him on a good day. Once permission was granted, I promised Mom I'd behave, and we went over the rules: No drinking. No smoking. No drugs. Don't go anywhere else. Call if there's any trouble.

Mom drove me to Terry's house. Before I got out of the car, I had to reassure her again. "Yes, Mom, I know the rules. If I need you, I'll call you."

Feeling a little nervous, I walked through the house into the garage that had been converted into a family rec room. I knew a few people from school, but there were just as many I didn't know. As I talked to Caroline, I noticed a young lady with bright-red hair sitting by herself near a corner of the garage. *Wow, she's beautiful!* I thought.

I couldn't imagine why she was sitting alone. *Did she have a boyfriend who would be back any minute? Will she even talk to me?* I decided to take a chance and at least say hi. Then the strobe light came on, and I tried to maneuver casually in her direction, which was not easy with the light flashing. Somehow, I managed to get close to her without falling over anything.

When the flashing stopped, and the regular lights came on, I could see her close up. Her hair was a golden red, her skin soft with light freckles. A hint of cleavage

## A Memoir of Finding Love Again

peaked above the curved neckline of her blouse. Her gentle smile encouraged me to start a conversation, so I commented about the strobe light.

It turned out she was good friends with Terry and Caroline. I told her I knew Caroline from French class. "I take French too," she said. Her smile inspired me to introduce myself to her in French. Her name was JoAnne, and though she spoke French with more ease than I did, my nervousness melted as we talked. I felt a comfortable connection like I had never felt before. We talked for most of the evening (in English), and was she nice!

*I'd like to get to know her better,* I said to myself.

Over the course of the next weeks and months, JoAnne and I spent a lot of time together. We went out on dates to the movies and to get pizza afterward, with Mom as our chauffeur. On weekends, Mom dropped me off at JoAnne's house. I helped with the gas money and listened to Mom's reminders as patiently as I could.

"I'm not ready for any grandchildren, so be a gentleman," Mom said. "If you go in any bedrooms, make sure the door stays open."

"Okay, Mom."

JoAnne's mom would knock after a few minutes of the bedroom door being closed. That was our cue to stop making out, though sometimes we really were just talking, and say, "Come in."

"Are you two okay? Would you like something to drink?"

# Trust the Timing

"We're okay, Thanks anyway."

"Why don't you take Lobo for a walk?"

Lobo was JoAnne's German shepherd. When he heard his name mentioned so close to the word *walk*, he pranced into the room with expectation, rushing to the door and then back to us, implying, *You heard the lady. Let's go for a walk!*

Doing stuff with Lobo was a treat for me. I'd always liked dogs, but up to this point, we weren't allowed to have one. "No dogs." It was as simple as that. I knew not to ask more than once, or I'd be sorry. I enjoyed throwing a ball around the backyard for Lobo or taking him for a walk around the neighborhood. Sometimes JoAnne and I would walk to the junior high school at night and make out on the bleachers while Lobo waited patiently and kept a lookout.

JoAnne and I talked honestly about sex and agreed there would be "no accidents." We didn't want sex to be something we would later regret. We were young, and it was not easy, but one of us would always be strong enough to say "stop" before things went too far. We had that level of respect for each other—though I did get my face slapped playfully once or twice, and I did get to explore second base on occasion.

On weekends when I didn't have to work, we hung around with Terry and Caroline, who lived in JoAnne's neighborhood. We'd sit around one of their living rooms listening mostly to James Taylor and Carole King, who

I got bored with. But one time Caroline found Black Sabbath's *Master of Reality* album in her brother's room when her parents were out.

"My mother would kill me if she knew we were playing this in the house," Caroline said as we listened to music more of my liking. I started carrying a case of eight-track tapes with me, so we could listen to Jethro Tull or Zeppelin. It was a great time in my life, hanging out with people who liked me for myself and didn't try to change me.

Somewhere around the beginning of 1972, my grandmother had another heart attack. She'd had three or four heart attacks over the past twenty years. One afternoon, I walked into the kitchen and saw Mom on the phone, crying.

"Okay, Dad. I love you," she said, trying to compose herself.

"What's wrong?" I asked.

"Grandma's in the hospital. She had another heart attack."

She didn't say too much more, but she was pretty upset. At the time, she and my father were not speaking much. He generally left early in the morning and didn't come home until very late at night. Mom felt alone and missed her parents. The move south wasn't working out the way she had hoped.

During spring break, Mom drove to Connecticut for

# Trust the Timing

a few days to see her parents. She took my two brothers while I stayed home with my father, so he could take me to work. Otherwise, I tried to stay out of his way as much as possible. Caroline and JoAnne picked me up to go to the movies or hang out when I was off.

A day or so after Mom came back, I got the announcement.

"We're going back to Connecticut at the end of the school year," my mother informed me.

I was devastated. I was just starting to make friends, I had my first real girlfriend, and now I had to move. Again. I didn't know how I would break this news to JoAnne.

Mom agreed to pick me up at JoAnne's house after school the next day, so I wouldn't have to ride the bus home. That way we would have some extra time together. As I walked JoAnne home, I tried to think of the best way to tell her. It was just under a mile to her house.

"Is something bothering you?" she asked about halfway there.

"Well, there is something, but I'd like to wait until we get to your house to talk about it," I said, trying to sound like it wasn't a big deal.

She frowned, searching for a response.

"How was your day?" I attempted.

"Bobby almost got me in trouble in French. Before the test, he was saying, 'Make sure I can see your paper.'" JoAnne rolled her eyes. "Then he kept clearing his throat and coughing during the test. Mrs. T. gave us that look where she raises one eyebrow."

"Did you let him see your paper?"

"Well, I didn't go out of my way. I wasn't about to make it obvious, so I tried to ignore him. But art class was great . . ."

JoAnne went on to talk about what she was working on in art and the people in her class. She loved art class. I tried to listen, which usually wasn't hard. But today was different.

When we got to her house, we went out back with Lobo. I threw the ball a couple of times for him, but my heart wasn't in it.

"What's wrong?" JoAnne asked.

I took a deep breath. "I have some bad news. We're moving. My family's going back to Connecticut. My grandma is sick, and Mom's worried about her. We're leaving as soon as school's out."

JoAnne looked stunned. As it started to sink in, her eyes filled with tears. I felt awful. There was nothing I could do but hold her.

We tried to spend as much time together as possible over the next few weeks. There were still a few good times, but it was hard for us to be happy with the move looming ahead. I held some resentment toward my parents during the process. It wasn't until years later that I understood how miserable my mother was in North Carolina. She was homesick, and her mother was dying.

## Trust the Timing

But at the time, I didn't realize how sick my grandma was. Mom hid that from us.

It was Friday, the twenty-eighth of May in 1972, the beginning of Memorial Day weekend, when we finalized the move. My mother and brothers had started out a couple of days earlier, leaving me to ride in the rental truck with my father. It was an emotional farewell with my friends, North Carolina, and most of all JoAnne.

At three in the afternoon, I kissed her goodbye, wondering if I would ever see her again. My father picked me up from school, and we were on the road by three thirty. If I'd had my way, I would have stayed, but I had no voice in that decision. Sadness wrapped around me as the truck turned onto US 17 and headed north.

# 3

## *JoAnne*

# The Moving Gremlin
## (1961–1972)

In 1972, when David told me he was moving, I didn't want to believe it. I wanted to throw up. It was another dirty trick the Moving Gremlin came up with to torment me. That little monster had disrupted my life too many times. I thought I was rid of him, but he was back again with an unexpected twist. I'd had my first taste of true love with a nice boy, and the Moving Gremlin was snatching him away from me.

Through much of my childhood, "we're moving" had been a dreaded, yet expected, announcement. By the age of twelve, I'd lived in eleven homes in eight different states plus Canada. I wanted more than anything to stay in one place, in a regular house with a big fenced-in backyard for the dog. A horse would be nice too. But being a military kid, I was grateful to be able to ride at the base stables and settled for sharing the yard with the whole neighborhood. I learned to adapt.

The first move I remember was to Newfoundland,

## Trust the Timing

Canada. We flew there from mom's hometown, Washington, DC, in 1961 to join Dad at the naval base at Argentia. The plane was small and the ride bumpy. Sitting between Mom and my big sister, Linda, I threw up in the airsick bag Mom handed me. She and Linda followed suit, each of them throwing up next to me. I think my baby sister, Mary Kaye, was the only one who didn't throw up on that flight.

Despite the miserable trip there, Newfoundland was a magical place with its blue icebergs and abundant snow, sledding down the hill in the backyard, and playing checkers with wood chips cut from the Christmas tree that had been too big to fit in the house until Dad cut it. French was the predominant language on the only TV station available, and while I only learned a few words, I'm glad for the early exposure to a different language. Even with their shopping flights to St. John's, Mom and her friends complained about living in such a remote location. She was happy with Dad's transfer back to the states a year later.

First, we went back to Washington. There, Dad bought a brand-new white '62 Chevrolet Biscayne with a red interior for the drive across the country to Camp Pendleton, California. My parents made a big deal about buying the amazing portable air-conditioner unit that attached to the top of the passenger window. Mom had to pull the chord to turn it on. We rode through the desert singing our version of "California Here I Come," changing the words to "right back where I never-been-before."

## A Memoir of Finding Love Again

Somewhere in the middle of the desert, the air conditioner stopped working. Mom pulled the cord, and nothing happened. Then Dad reached across and gave the cord a yank, and the air conditioner went crazy, spitting ice water everywhere and making Mom shriek.

Back then, moving was still an adventure.

Dad's assignment to Camp Pendleton turned out to be the longest I'd live in one place for a while. I got to go to the same school for *three whole years*. I had no idea what a luxury that would become. Linda, who Dad had adopted from Mom's first marriage, was ten years older than me. She fell in love with a corporal who worked as a projectionist at the base movie theater, and they got married when she was sixteen.

I was just finishing up third grade when I found out it was time to move again.

We said goodbye to Linda and traveled back across the country to Pennsylvania. When we got to our new home, in a suburb outside of Philadelphia, I couldn't find the twenty or so stuffed animals that had shared my bed in California. They weren't in any of the boxes that came off the moving van.

"They must have gotten lost on the trip," Mom said. "I'm sorry, honey. We'll get you some new ones."

At nine years old, I knew they were just stuffed animals, sort of. But I'd had them for a big chunk of my life, and most of them had names. The Moving Gremlin must have gotten them. That became the safest explanation. It didn't occur to me that one of my parents might have purposely thrown them away.

Dad was stationed at the Philadelphia naval base where he served as the brig warden for a year until he shipped out to Vietnam. The week before Dad left, I got into a book-bag "fight" with a girl while walking home from the Catholic school I went to for three months. She had long blonde hair that fell in ringlets. Back then, in fifth grade, our book bags were like small suitcases. Imagine two ten-year-old girls in blue-and-green plaid skirts and white blouses swinging our book bags at each other. I used mine mostly as a shield. I'm not sure how it started, but I was not a fighter, so *she* must have started it—must have said mean and nasty things to me. Maybe there was some hair pulling too. What I recall most is how my dad reacted when I got home.

"What's wrong?" Dad asked from his recliner. He must have seen the tear trails on my face. I told him what had happened. "Come here," he said gently. He then picked me up and held me on his lap for a long time. I couldn't remember him doing that before, though I'm sure he did when I was a baby because there are photos. To this day, I remember the feeling of being utterly safe and protected in my father's arms as all my fears melted away.

Mom must have felt that sense of safety and comfort from Dad even more than I did. She must have depended on his strength, because when Dad was in Vietnam, the depression she'd struggled with in California got worse.

## A Memoir of Finding Love Again

When I was eight, Mom had been hospitalized and given "shock treatment" while my little sister and I stayed with another family for two weeks. Mom was a bit confused for a while after that. Before Dad left for Vietnam, he told us, "You need to be patient with your mother. She might have trouble remembering things because of the shock treatment."

Mom missed Dad terribly the year he was in Vietnam. She didn't drive and depended on friends to take her to the store and to the doctor. To be closer to family, we moved from Philadelphia to Michigan to stay with Linda and her husband for three months. Then we moved to New York to stay with another military family we knew from Camp Pendleton.

That was also the year I entered puberty. At the age of eleven, my body was changing so much, I felt it didn't belong to me anymore. It was like I woke up one morning with two melons attached to my chest. They got in the way of everything, kept outgrowing their harness, and messed up my center of gravity. To cope with all the confusion of not knowing whose body I was walking around in, not knowing what condition my mother would be in, and not knowing when we might move next, I was drawn to things I could control. I did well in school, made up stories in my head, and watched a lot of TV in the bedroom I shared with Mom and Mary Kaye.

*Star Trek* was my favorite show, and Spock was my first crush. He was so rational and dependable. I envied

## Trust the Timing

his ability to suppress his emotions. His intelligence encouraged me to work harder in school and reinforced my interest in science. Mary Kaye, on the other hand, did not do so well in school. She was a free spirit and better at making friends, which was never my strong suit. Mom called her "the happy-go-lucky one." I guess I was the serious one.

When there was nothing good on TV, I spent a lot of my free time sitting with Hoppy in his doghouse. Hoppy was a Newfoundland shepherd mix, a large dog with long black hair with tan underneath and on his muzzle. Dad got him from one of his buddies in California, who named him Hoppy because he would leap up and down at the end of his chain when he was happy to see someone.

Hoppy had been a loyal companion, making all the trips with us since California. In New York, Hoppy had to be chained up to his doghouse outside. When things felt unbearable, I would retreat there. It was our little cave where I would sit and talk with my quiet friend and fantasize about being a brave heroine who saved the planet. Sometimes I fantasized about simple things, like living in a house with a big fenced-in backyard for Hoppy like he had for a couple of months when we stayed with Linda in Michigan. I hated for him to be on a chain. I took him for walks occasionally, but he was a strong dog, and I didn't want him to get away from me in a strange place.

One morning I woke up, and Hoppy was gone. No

one knew how he got loose or what had happened to him. When he didn't come back that night, I was distraught with worry. A few days later he did come back, to my great joy and relief, but he disappeared again the next day while I was at school. When I got home, my mom told me a story.

"When Hoppy got lost the first time, he found a very sick little girl, and she fell in love with him," Mom began. "The little girl had to go to the hospital, and she said Hoppy was the only thing that would make her better, so we gave Hoppy to her."

"When can he come back home?" I asked. "When she gets better?"

"I don't know. She's really sick," Mom said. "They are even letting Hoppy lay next to her bed in the hospital. They can't get him to leave her. He knows she's sick and that she needs him."

My stomach felt tight, and I wanted to cry. Hoppy was my best friend. I could talk to him any time, and he listened to me. He was the only one who understood me.

*I need him too!* I thought. But I didn't say it.

"They're taking good care of him," Mom added. "And they have a big backyard he can run around in."

I felt confused and worried, but the part of me that was good at adapting got me to believe the story, like when my stuffed-animal menagerie got lost in the move, only this was more serious. I could make the sacrifice if the sick little girl needed Hoppy more than I did and

## Trust the Timing

if they were going to take good care of him. I knew if I asked more questions, it would make things harder for Mom, and I didn't want to do that. Years later, I wondered about the sick-little-girl story, but I was afraid to dig too deep, afraid of what I might find out. To this day, thinking about Hoppy brings a stony ache to my heart. Of all the dogs I've ever lost, Hoppy is the one I most long to see in heaven.

Soon after Hoppy disappeared, we moved again—this time to Quantico, Virginia, to stay with another military family for the summer. Our new host family included three teenagers, the youngest two being boys. It was awkward, to say the least. Mom had another nervous breakdown and went to the hospital for a few days. The boys made goofy sexual gestures, like the time the younger boy danced into our bedroom (it had probably been their bedroom before we came) wearing only a towel, and his brother grabbed the towel away. We only had a quick glimpse. After a stunned second, the boys started wrestling. I pretended to go back to reading my book as if I didn't care, and they took their antics elsewhere. It could have been worse. We were safe. We had a roof over our heads and food to eat. I still had *Star Trek* and my books. But I longed to live in a house with just my family.

Later that summer, we found out Dad would be stationed at Camp Lejeune after Vietnam, so we moved into base housing at Tarawa Terrace to wait for him. After

## A Memoir of Finding Love Again

Dad came home, things felt more normal. My parents did a good job of hiding the challenges they faced together. It wasn't until many years later that I would learn about the torment that haunted Dad from doing time in Vietnam.

With Dad home, I felt a sense of stability and freedom to heed my "tomboy" callings to explore the nearby woods with my new dog. I'd discovered Lobo when I was walking home from school, cutting through the duplexes. He was a few months old, mostly tan, with a shepherd look around his black muzzle, and he was barking from the end of his chain so I stopped to pet him. After a couple of minutes, a lady came out of the house.

"Do you want him?" she asked.

I was stunned by her offer, not sure what to say.

"My husband brought him home, but he barks too much and chews on everything."

"Sure, I want him!" I said. *Who wouldn't want a cool dog like this?* "But I have to ask my parents."

Mom and Dad gave in to my heartfelt begging, and I brought Lobo home the next day. With Dad home *and* a dog, our family felt whole again.

In 1969, it was time for Dad to retire from the Marine Corps. I learned years later that he'd been tempted to accept a promotion to master sergeant, but Mom convinced him that the pay increase wasn't worth another tour in Vietnam.

Mom and Dad were talking about going back to

## Trust the Timing

Pennsylvania. My last memories of that state included the Catholic school in Philadelphia right before Dad left to go to war. I wanted to stay in North Carolina, and I whined about it often. I liked staying in one place and knowing where things were. I liked romping through the woods with Lobo in the afternoons and riding horses at the base stables on Saturday mornings with my friends. I'd had enough of being the new kid in a strange place.

One day before the move, we were driving around running errands, getting ready for the trip north. I was in the back seat worrying.

"Is it *impossible* for us to stay in North Carolina?" I asked.

"Nothing is impossible," Dad stated. He said it in that clear philosophical tone he used when he wanted me to remember something my whole life.

That shut me up for a while and gave me something to think about.

I grabbed hold of his words and held onto the thread of hope that it was *possible* for us to stay in North Carolina.

We actually made it to Pennsylvania, but the deal fell through on the house we were going to buy. The guy who was supposed to build a house for the people we were buying from took their money and went to Mexico, so there was no house available for us to move into. I could tell Dad was disgusted. He never used profanity in front of us kids, but I could almost see the curse words stewing in his head. He called the moving company and found out our furniture was still in North Carolina. (Maybe there were other forces at work besides the Moving Gremlin.)

"Maybe we should just go back to North Carolina," Mom said. "I never really wanted to leave there anyway."

"Well, Betty, why didn't you say so?" Dad asked.

Mom shrugged. "Well, Jim, you wanted to come back to Pennsylvania."

I couldn't believe my luck! We headed back down south, reinforcing the magical belief in my adolescent brain that anything *is* possible.

Going from junior high on a military base to a public school in Jacksonville, North Carolina, only a short distance away, was ironically like going to a different part of the world. Not having a noticeable accent made me a minority. Race had never seemed like a big deal living in the melting pot of base schools and military housing. My mom was always talking about how it didn't make any difference what color a person's skin was. But in the civilian South, there was a separateness between blacks and whites I had not experienced before. Black and white kids generally lived in different neighborhoods, and they sat at different tables in the school cafeteria. I didn't see much interaction between people of different races. Most of my classmates had lived in North Carolina their whole lives, and some had been friends since childhood. All these things were foreign concepts to me.

## Trust the Timing

Then there were the regular paddlings by teachers. I'd never heard of teachers paddling students, not even in Catholic school—though I wonder if they were just quieter about it. At my new school, we heard the swat, swat, swat out in the hallway at least once a week. It was mostly boys who got paddled. But there were exceptions. The red-faced, overweight teacher I had for study hall paddled everyone in her class who admitted to talking while she was out of the room. I had said maybe three words while she was out, but fear dominated my usual honesty. I wasn't about to subject myself to the humiliation of physical assault over a few quiet words. The possibility of being hit with a paddle reinforced the shyness of being in a new school where teachers were unpredictable and it wasn't safe to talk in class.

Despite the unexpected cultural changes, I was glad we didn't have to move so far away and that we got a house with a big fenced-in backyard for Lobo. I adapted and finally started to make solid friendships that would carry over into high school and beyond.

My closest girlfriends, Terry and Sally, came from military families and, like me, had lived in other states. Later we met Caroline, who taught me how to play the guitar. We listened to the Beatles, Melanie's *Candles in the Rain*, and Carole King's *Tapestry* album. We walked to the movie theater or rode our bikes to the Dairy Queen and wondered if we were ever going to have boyfriends . . .

## A Memoir of Finding Love Again

The boyfriend came along in the beginning of tenth grade and opened up a world of new, exciting emotions. Everything seemed perfect. I loved David, and he loved me back. We were so happy. And then suddenly, out of nowhere, he was *moving!* It was so unfair! We wouldn't even have any of the summer together.

Looking back, that was probably a good thing. It would have been even harder to resist our natural desires on hot summer nights after a day at the beach seeing each other in swimsuits—in all that bare skin—with all those hormones. Who knows where that road might have taken us?

But at sixteen, I felt like my world was falling apart. I had never been in love before, and I couldn't imagine there being anyone else but David. I remember crying a lot, especially when certain sad songs came on the radio, like Harry Nilsson's anguished "Without You." I'd look at David with this sad puppy-dog face, and he'd look back at me like, *I'm sorry. I can't do anything about this.*

"You know," Mom said, "your crying so much is just making it harder for David. He doesn't have a choice."

"You just don't understand!" I wailed.

"Yes, I do understand," she said quietly.

It slowly dawned on me that someone might have told her the same thing about her tears when Dad was getting ready to go to Vietnam. I remembered what it was like having to move just when things were getting settled, just as I was getting comfortable with people. So

## Trust the Timing

I worked on not crying so much, but I still felt like my heart was going to break.

One afternoon, David and I were sitting with his mother at the Dairy Queen having ice cream and listening to a young Michael Jackson sing "I'll Be There" on the radio. Toward the end of the song, there's the part about how any future boyfriend better treat you right, or else . . .

"I'll bust him in the head," David interjected quietly.

I put my hands over my face, but I couldn't stop the tears. David was willing to be my knight in shining armor. But he was leaving! He reached out to hold my hand, and his mom gave me a napkin. There wasn't much anyone could say.

We said our goodbyes on the last day of school. Most of the students had already sprinted off into summer vacation. David and I drug our feet toward the parking lot where his father waited in the truck. We stopped on the breezeway near the office.

The tears swam in my eyes, but somehow I managed to keep them from spilling out as I looked up at him. "Do you think we'll ever see each other again?"

"I hope so." David hugged me and gave me one last kiss. "I love you," he said. Then he stood up straight. "I have to go now."

"I love you, too." Part of me wanted to hold onto him, beg him not to leave, make him promise to come back. But that would just make it harder. "Promise you'll write

## A Memoir of Finding Love Again

to me so I have your address, okay?"

"I promise." His eyes told me he would. Then he walked to the truck.

I couldn't watch him leave without crying, so I started the walk home and let the tears roll down my cheeks. David was leaving North Carolina. By that night, he would be so far away, like the Carole King song.

I got a letter a couple of weeks later. It was mostly small talk about where they were staying with "Love Always, Dave" at the end. Over the next couple of months, I wrote four letters to David, and he wrote twice. I did some babysitting that summer, mostly for a couple with three children. It wasn't really babysitting because the kids ranged from six to ten years old and just needed someone older to keep an eye on them when their parents worked. The mom felt like a big sister to me. I think she'd been a Marine Corps wife and knew about being apart from the one you love. I told her about my boyfriend moving away and how sad I was.

"If you and David are meant to be together, then you will be," she said with certainty.

"But I don't know how that would happen."

"I know. But if it's meant to be, then it will be. If not, you'll still be okay."

It was a simple statement of faith, different from other people telling me to move on with my life. It helped me believe things would work out, one way or another.

## Trust the Timing

There were times later in high school and in college when I'd see a tall, slender young man with blonde hair who reminded me of David, and my heart would skip a beat as I did a double take. Memories of my first love faded over the years, but those memories remained the sweetest ever. He was a good first boyfriend. No one else would ever love me with that kind of respectfully restrained passion.

4

*David*

# Moving On
## (1972–1973)

It was hard to leave JoAnne and North Carolina, but it was good to see family and friends again. For the first few months, we lived with another family, longtime friends of my parents, and it was a little crowded until we found our own rental. A full-time job at the motorcycle shop down the road got me out of the house and kept me busy for the summer.

With working and hanging out with friends, JoAnne was becoming a pleasant but distant memory. For the first few weeks, family and friends kept telling me, "You're here and she's there. It's time to move on," and "You'll both move on. She's probably already got another boyfriend."

*They could be right*, I thought. I couldn't blame her if she did find another boyfriend. I'd written her a couple of letters and thought about calling her, but long-distance calls were out of the question. My parents didn't want me adding to our host family's phone bill. Plus, living with eight other people in a three-bedroom house meant there was practically no privacy. So, at the young age of fifteen, with JoAnne seven hundred miles away, I listened to the wisdom of family. I moved on to live in the present.

My brothers and I raised all sorts of Cain that summer, riding motorcycles through nearby fields and throwing firecrackers. It was typical for adults to sit outside in the evenings sipping beer or just talking. We were old enough now to be accepted by the adults who began to include us in conversations. It was kind of fun just hanging around the neighborhood.

In early September, it was time to return to the same high school I had left eighteen months prior. Walking into school the first day was a homecoming of sorts and something new at the same time. There were some new faces among the faculty and students, and yet, in some ways, it was like I had never left. Still, with the moves came academic challenges. The Connecticut school system didn't accept North Carolina's math curriculums, so it was back to taking algebra 1, which was quite frustrating and disheartening, to say the least. *Here we go again.*

"You'll look back at high school as the best years of your life," adults told me. But I hated sitting in a classroom, listening to the same old drudge every day. I felt stifled. I wanted to be working. Still, I somehow got motivated to do better academically than I had before just so I could get it behind me.

As the school year progressed, I did the typical things, like studying for my driver's license and hanging out with friends like David Kruz who lived across town. He'd come pick me up, and we'd play cards at his house with his father and brother and a few other guys. We played a lot of eight-hand pitch on Saturday nights. There was no booze, which was okay. I figured out later that Mr. Kruz was playing cards with us to keep us off the street.

Around midyear, my focus started to shift away from studying. The frustrations of repeating many of my classes moved toward discontent. My English teacher, Mr. Graves, and I did not see eye to eye. We had several discussions about my performance during the first semester. But the harder I worked, the more difficult the environment became. We had to write essays about literature, and the grading was subjective. I felt like no matter what I did, it would not be good enough.

"What do I have to do to pass this class?" I asked him.

"You're just not working hard enough" was his response. I felt like I was working my butt off. The discontent moved toward rebellion.

Poetry and the literary "classics" were of no interest to me. Give me a sentence to diagram, and I could do it with no problem, but *The Great Gatsby* made me sick to the point of nausea. I suffered through the first two chapters and decided I'd had enough of snooty people I had nothing in common with. Unfortunately, I still had

## Trust the Timing

to hear about them during class discussions. One day, my irritation spilled over.

"Why do we gotta read this crap?" I blurted out.

Mr. Graves looked at me with disdain. "Get out!" he ordered. "Go to the office. *Now.*"

I sat in the office for the rest of the class period, which was fine with me. Then Graves went in and told the principal I was swearing in his class. When the principal found out I had said the word *crap*, he counseled me to use a better choice of words and to not be disrespectful to Mr. Graves. I made sure I didn't say anything in class after that. All I did was take up space.

While school bored the hell out of me, learning to drive offered a chance at independence. On weekends, I practiced driving with Mom. She was a good teacher, being patient and not yelling at me too much. My driving test ended up being at four o'clock on a Friday afternoon. It took less than ten minutes. I was prepared to do everything I'd practiced, but all I had to do was go down the road and do a three-point turn, and I had my license.

That May, I started working after school at Polardi's gas station across from a truck stop near Hwy 95. The job got me out of the house and reinforced the principles I'd been taught: work hard, and if you want more, work more.

At Polardi's, I pumped gas and got to learn about engines, which was much more interesting than Mr. Graves's classics. It came as no surprise that I ended up failing English for the year. Summer school was a joke. There were six other people in the class. All we had to do was read *Bless the Beasts and Children* and discuss it during class—no tests, no essays. I just had to show up for three hours in the morning, then Mom picked me up and took me to work.

My job provided much needed cash toward a car of my own and an escape from the challenges at home. I guess my parents hoped that moving to a new house would make everything better. They had a four-bedroom house built on a big wooded lot in the country, and we moved in during the summer of '73. It was nice to have my own room and a little more privacy. For a while, the new house did provide some distraction from the underlying domestic tension. But within a few weeks the usual stress returned, thick as ever, with noticeable discord and periodic ranting, mostly from my father. I tried to get away as much as possible by going to friends' houses or getting my parents to let me use their car to go somewhere, anywhere.

Adding to the stress at home, my grandma's health was deteriorating. In April of '73, she'd been diagnosed with advanced abdominal cancer, but I think she knew long before then. Coronary artery disease had worn her out. But that didn't stop her from making comments about my hair being too long. And she continued to be an avid reader. She always had a book on her dining room table and talked to my mother about what she was reading. When Grandma was young, she loved to travel to far and distant places with friends. One summer they went southwest to California. Another year they drove to Alaska.

Grampa Malcolm, however, didn't like to travel much. Back when I was just a kid, he'd come visit us for dinner and report: "The old woman's off with her friends again." He always had a twinkle in his eye when he called her "the old woman." He missed her, but he was glad she was enjoying herself. During his visits, he told us stories about growing up in the early 1900s and supporting his sisters after his parents died, and how, at fifteen, he got a job with the railroad until they found out his age and let him go. After that, he worked whatever odd jobs he could to keep his sisters from going to an orphanage. I always admired his determination to keep his family together and came to believe that if I could be half the man my grandfather was, I'd do well.

My grandparents had different interests, but I could tell they liked each other. They had a comfortable way of bantering between them, which was fun to watch. When Grampa said something a little off-color or used profanity, Grandma gave him a sharp, "Malcolm!" Grampa then gave us an "ooh, I got caught" look and grinned. They had their squabbles, but they had their laughs too and enjoyed each other's company. After retirement, they had five good years together and took short trips to Massachusetts or Cape Cod, or "leaf peepin" in New Hampshire.

## A Memoir of Finding Love Again

In August of 1973, it was my honor to drive my grandmother home from the hospital to be with my grandfather before she died. Mom asked me to drive for her, and at sixteen, I was proud to be able to help. I didn't know that it would be the last time we would see Grandma alive. She was exhausted by four in the afternoon when we got her home to her recliner in their living room.

I was still awake when I heard the phone ring in Mom's bedroom a little after midnight.

"Okay, Daddy, I'll be there shortly."

I knew by the softness of Mom's voice that Grandma was gone.

By the time she got off the phone, I was dressed and in the hallway outside her room, ready to go. My father was downstairs on the couch with the TV on.

"I'll drive," I said.

"Thank you."

"Are you alright?" I asked.

"I guess so," she answered.

We got there as they were taking Grandma's body out on a gurney to the hearse. Mom and I went inside to be with Grampa. He sat quietly in his recliner next to Grandma's empty recliner. Mom and I sat on the couch. We listened to the clock ticking.

"I laid down next to her on the bed," he began. "She told me she saw stars. Then she couldn't see anything. She felt some pain, and she said, 'Oh, God.' Then she was gone."

# Trust the Timing

I didn't know what emotions to feel. But I thought about how my grandparents' home had always been my sanctuary. I remembered Grandma teaching me how to make pies on Thanksgiving eve when I was ten years old and Mom volunteered my services. We made apple pies, squash pies, mincemeat pies, pumpkin pies, and orange marmalade. I peeled and cut up the fruit and then Grandma showed me how to roll out piecrust and make cranberry relish and mincemeat with the old hand grinder. After the baking was done, I got to watch The *March of the Wooden Soldiers,* an old 1930s Laurel and Hardy movie, with my grandparents. We had lots of laughs at the slapstick antics of the nutcrackers. For twenty-four whole hours, I felt like an only child on vacation. Thanksgiving eve with Mom's parents had been a holiday tradition I looked forward to.

My grandparents provided a cohesive anchor for my family and gave me a healthier perspective of marriage compared to the one I saw with my own parents. Except for the year we lived in North Carolina, they had always been a big part of my life. Coming back to Connecticut reunited us at a crucial time when I had no idea then how much I would come to value the times I spent with Malcolm and Edna Leonard.

5

*JoAnne*

# Save the Whales!
(1972–1977)

During the summer between tenth and eleventh grade, Terry and I rode our bikes everywhere. By everywhere, I mean the Dairy Queen, the movies, the whole North Woods Park neighborhood, and the shopping center where we spent our babysitting money on record albums, clothes, makeup, and posters. Sally rode with us sometimes, when she wasn't mingling with the coolest of the hippies and freaks at Mystic Arts, the head shop downtown where her older sister knew everybody. Caroline, when she wasn't dating or working at her parents' dry-cleaning business, drove us to the arcade or the bowling alley where we played foosball and air hockey.

One warm summer night, Terry and I were cruising the neighborhood on our bikes and passed two guys riding bikes in the opposite direction. They turned around and came up beside us.

"Hey, ya mind if we ride along?" asked the one with short dark hair.

## Trust the Timing

"Okay, as long as you don't try anything funny," Terry answered.

"He's the funny one," he said, motioning to his friend with long blonde hair.

"No, I'm the smart one."

They were both tall and nice looking. Aside from their hair color, they looked like they could be related.

"Are you two brothers?" I asked.

"No, we're cousins," said the blonde. We found out a couple of weeks later it was a running joke.

It turned out that the younger "cousin," Rick, with the short hair, lived the next block over from me. Tom, who was a few years older than all of us, lived a few blocks away, closer to Terry. We started hanging out together, riding our bikes around the neighborhood. Tom and Rick would meet us at Terry's house or my house, and we'd ride to the high school or the DQ and talk.

One night, Tom asked, "Hey, what do you guys think about us all going out on a date?"

"Hmmm, we might need to think about that," Terry said. She was still holding out for a juvenile delinquent she'd gone out with a couple of times. The next day, Terry and I put our heads together and came up with a counteroffer. Caroline wasn't seeing anyone seriously, so we called and asked her if she was interested, which she was. Then Terry called Tom and told him she was seeing someone, but that Caroline and I would like to go out with him and Rick.

## A Memoir of Finding Love Again

At this point, we were all just friends. Caroline hadn't met the "cousins," so she asked which one I wanted to be with. Tom was older, already out of high school, and since Caroline was generally the most mature one in our bunch, I reasoned that she should sit with Tom who would be driving. Besides, I knew from our conversations that Rick was more outdoorsy. He had a certain air of friendly confidence about him and a nice big smile.

The Saturday afternoon before the double date, I looked through my earrings and beads and noticed the ring David had given me. I hadn't made a conscious decision to stop wearing it. I'd just been leaving it on the dresser lately. As I studied the blue stone, a ripple of sadness passed through me. David had not answered my last two letters. It had been at least a month since I'd heard anything from him. *If he cared about me, he would have written me back by now. He must be interested in other things, or maybe other people.* That hurt my feelings a little, but now, here was Rick. I placed David's ring in a drawer and put on my gold gypsy earrings.

Caroline drove over to my house, and Tom and Rick picked us up at around six thirty in Tom's old Chevy Impala. I got in the back with Rick; Caroline rode up front. The guys both worked at the movie theater, so we all got in free and had free popcorn and drinks. After the movie, Rick said, "Let's go to the cemetery!" At nine thirty at night, this sounded like an adventure, and we all agreed.

The old, wooded cemetery was near a shopping

center where we left the car. With the guys' help, we easily climbed over a sagging part of the chain-link fence. It was almost too dark to see, which made it funny and spooky at the same time. Rick led the way, taking my hand as we followed the winding path around the graves and left Caroline and Tom behind. Then we stopped near a large tree. I could almost see Rick's warm smile in the darkness. His kiss felt natural and exciting, full of confidence.

Rick was playful yet industrious. When he wasn't working at the movies, he washed cars and did yard work for money to restore the rusty old Jeep sitting in his parents' backyard. Rick's way of asking me out on a date was to say, "If you come help me with this yard, we can ride our bikes up to the steak house and have dinner." I'd heard about women's liberation, so I didn't mind helping out with the yard work. It seemed only natural.

After school started, Rick cut back on working at the movies to play sports, and I took over some of his shifts at the movie theater, the same movie theater where David and I used to go. I thought of David now and then. Sweet, considerate David. There had still been no word from him, so I felt sure he had another girlfriend.

Rick and I dated through my junior and senior year. He was a pretty good boyfriend. He was only trying to be helpful when he suggested I run more to get rid of the little bit of cellulite in my thighs and that doing push-ups would firm up my less-than-perfect breasts.

## A Memoir of Finding Love Again

After he finished restoring the Jeep, he put up curtains in the back, which provided privacy for our enthusiastic explorations into what teenagers sometimes explored in the nights of drive-in movies—besides the movies.

We were young, healthy, and full of life. On Saturdays in the summer, we'd get up around five in the morning to go to the beach. It was still dark when Rick took his fishing pole and tackle box out to the pier. I'd often sit with him and watch the sunrise before going back to sleep in the back of the Jeep until a reasonable hour. Then I'd get up, and we'd go for a swim. Once we got a natural high by swimming all the way out to the end of the pier.

Natural highs were the predominant ones back then. Rick and I occasionally indulged in a bottle of Strawberry Hill Boones Farm while Terry and Sally gravitated to more liberal crowds and indulgences. We were still friends but didn't see each other as much, traveling in different circles. Tom moved to Wilmington, North Carolina, to go to college, but we still saw him now and then. Caroline, who easily found a new boyfriend, taught me a few more guitar chords. I learned to play "One Tin Soldier" (the theme from *Billy Jack*), "Blowin' in the Wind," and other folksy ballads. John Denver's "Rocky Mountain High" reinforced my love for nature. Almost everything I wore was green, including my woven Sagittarius purse. I had this green-and-white T-shirt of the ecology flag that looked good on me, so I wore that a lot. In my senior

## Trust the Timing

year, in spite of natural talents in art and French, I started thinking about majoring in biology so I could help save the planet, or at least the whales. I was sure I'd go to college since I liked school and worked hard for good grades.

My sister Mary Kaye, on the other hand, skipped school a lot. She was the rebellious wild child and even quit going to school for a while because she despised one of her teachers. I was the conscientious one who hung out with brainy nerds and dated a jock. Being so different, Mary Kaye and I used to bicker a lot.

I'd been accepted at a college in the North Carolina mountains, which seemed like a perfect fit with my love for nature. I felt confident about my decision to go there—confident in my academic abilities, anyway. On the morning I was getting ready to leave, I was surprised when Mary Kaye got up early to hug me goodbye. It felt strange but sweet. *Maybe I should have been nicer to her. Maybe I should have helped her with schoolwork more.* But I tucked that thought away and focused on the transition ahead.

I found myself crying as we loaded my stuff into Dad's station wagon. The crying took me by surprise. Though I hadn't moved in five years, it wasn't like I hadn't lived plenty of other places. When I got to Boone, I unpacked and met my roommate. She was a pretty blonde and nice enough, but I started to feel more and more out of place. I hadn't even started classes but felt like the new kid in a new school again. On top of that, I wasn't sure how I was going to finance college beyond the small scholarship that took care of the first semester's tuition and board, and there were unexpected expenses for books. I didn't like asking my parents for help. My academic skills were good, but my practical problem-solving and social skills were apparently lacking. I felt overwhelmed and missed Rick, who'd been my boyfriend for two years.

On my second day in Boone, before classes started, my roommate and I went to a pub not far from campus. I recognized Chris, a superbrainy girl from my high school who'd already been at the college for a year. We'd been more acquaintances than friends, and I'd always felt a little intimidated by her intelligence and the fact that she'd had a thing for Rick before I met him. She waved to me and invited us to sit with her. My roommate saw some people she knew and went to sit with them. Chris made me feel welcome, and I started to feel comfortable with her. Maybe the beer helped. She asked me how I was doing.

"Well, I'm a little nervous," I admitted.

"That's normal. It'll get better."

"And I miss Rick. I'm actually thinking of going back home."

Chris looked thoughtful. "You know, you've got your whole life to go to college," she said. "If you want to go home, it's okay. It's your decision."

I was surprised by her response. I'd expected her to

encourage me to stay. If this brainiac said it was okay to go home, then who was I to fight it any longer?

I called my parents and said I wanted to come home. Having just driven seven hours each way to bring me there a couple of days earlier, Dad refused to come get me. He didn't say much, leading me to guess he was disgusted or at least disappointed. It wasn't until decades later that I found out Dad didn't come get me because he'd had car trouble on the way home, and money was tight. Very tight. I had no idea they were having financial problems back then. I figured it was all about not wanting to bail me out when I should have stayed.

Being stubborn, I was determined to find a way home. I called Rick, who was still a senior in high school and had to work, or had football practice or something. He sounded annoyed. Maybe he was disappointed too.

Looking back, I still wonder why I didn't just stay and figure things out. Sure, I missed my boyfriend. Sure, I was insecure and confused. But I was supposed to be smart, and I was smart—*academically*. But something was obviously missing.

I must have been feeling desperate because I called the movie theater where I'd worked to ask if anyone could help me get home.

Edward, who worked as a projectionist at another theater, volunteered to come get me. I knew Edward as part of the crowd who worked in the same chain of movie theaters. He seemed like a nice, responsible guy.

## A Memoir of Finding Love Again

He bought a bike rack to carry my ten-speed on his car and even paid for separate motel rooms for us before the drive back to Jacksonville.

Walking back into my parents' house, I felt hugely disappointed in myself and confused by my own behavior. Everyone, including me, had expected that I'd be successful in college. And here I was coming back like a homesick puppy. The transition into adulthood was going to be a rocky and twisted road.

Though my official reason for coming back home was that I missed Rick, within a couple of weeks I ended up dating Edward, who'd asked me out soon after coming to my rescue. He fed my romantic side, opening doors for me and paying for our dinner instead of going "dutch" like Rick preferred. Edward smoked cigarettes and had his own apartment. Being with him felt more grown up and more serious, at least on the surface. Unfortunately, besides the fact that we worked for the same movie-theater chain, Edward and I didn't have a lot in common. Important differences were clarified by the movie *The Stepford Wives*, which I watched multiple times. My consciousness was being raised while he claimed, in a semi-joking way, to like the idea of a perfect, submissive wife, even if she was a robot. The relationship was doomed yet managed to drag on and off for two years. We were not what we each wanted the other to be, but we kept hoping.

The turmoil that came from dating someone who was

## Trust the Timing

not a good fit distracted me from my own goals. A mild depression came over me and thwarted my attempts to go to the local community college. I didn't always make it to class. After a while, I just quit going and settled for selling tickets at the movie theater.

One afternoon, I sat alone in my room watching leaf shadows fluttering on the curtain. Feeling bored and restless, I picked up my guitar from the corner and wiped away the dust. My fingers tried to remember something. The simple chords from the *Billy Jack* theme song came back as I sang "One Tin Soldier." The first time I had seen that movie was with David. Things were so much simpler back when I was sixteen and with David, who kissed like heaven and loved me just the way I was. It felt like such a long time ago. *He's probably married by now,* I thought.

Meanwhile, my sister was having issues of her own. Mary Kaye was still technically enrolled in high school, though she didn't attend very often. Much to our dad's displeasure, she was dating a guy in his early twenties with hair almost down to his waist. She smoked cigarettes, and who knows what else, and often bummed money off people. At one point, she ran away from home and stayed gone for a few days. Mom and Dad were relieved to see her when she came back. I was annoyed that she had worried them so much, but I didn't say anything to her.

Though Mary Kaye had a rebellious nature, she had a

## A Memoir of Finding Love Again

kind heart. Once a week, she changed out of her ragged jeans and bandanna headband to put on her yellow-and-white "candy striper" uniform to volunteer at Carobell, a home for severely handicapped children. Mary Kaye loved to take care of the children at Carobell, especially the hydrocephalic boy who needed his huge head turned regularly.

One day, Mom showed me Mary Kaye's report card. Her French teacher, Mrs. T., whose class I had done well in, wrote a note that Mary Kaye should have ample help at home with French. That was my cue to begin tutoring my sister. We'd sit in the living room and make flash cards for French.

"So why don't you like school?" I asked her.

"I don't mind French and history, but I hate my math teacher. She talks to me like I'm an idiot."

"Maybe you can switch to a different class. Ask the guidance counselor."

"Maybe. I'll think about it. But I'm not smart like you. School is hard for me."

"Well, I'm not perfect, you know. I had to work hard at school."

"Yeah, I know you're not perfect. You date nerds."

I saw the hint of a smile and couldn't help but smile back. It had been a long time since I'd had a real conversation with my little sister. I rolled my eyes. "Edward's not a nerd. He's a . . . business man."

"That's even worse."

## Trust the Timing

Though I didn't agree with her lifestyle, the tutoring led to us talking more—about school and her work at Carobell and what she wanted to do with her life. She thought she might want to be a nurse or work with animals. There were moments when it seemed we were even starting to *like* each other again.

On the night of her sixteenth birthday, Mary Kaye and her boyfriend went out to celebrate. They were meeting their friends at The Brooklyn Spaghetti House. Dad called the owner, Mr. Carbone, who agreed to charge everything to Dad's account and assured him there would be no liquor. But Mary Kaye never made it to the restaurant. Less than a half a mile before they got there, their car was hit by a drunk driver. My little sister and her boyfriend were killed on their way to celebrate her sixteenth birthday.

That night, I watched Dad working to hold himself together and shaking his head in disbelief. He held a burning cigarette between his fingers for the first time in many years. It was frightening to see my dad like that, even for just a few moments.

Aside from worrying about my parents' reactions, I was numb with disbelief about losing my sister. It was too awful. My own grief would take years to process, years for it to sink in that my family had been brutally robbed. We would never get to see my sister work through her challenges and become the loving adult she could have been. I would never get to enjoy the special bond with my sister that would have developed over the years if she had lived.

Things got more confusing after Mary Kaye died. I lost track of who I was. Many years later, a counselor friend suggested I had adopted my sister's traits as a way of grieving for her. The lost child within me latched onto my sister's rebellious scapegoat persona, and together, our identities usurped the wounded hero. That would be a convenient excuse for all the drinking and partying I did after her death. I floundered without much sense of direction. In my early twenties, I started smoking cigarettes, which was way out of character for me—I had gotten all over Mary Kaye's case about smoking. In times of despair, I even had passing thoughts of walking in front of a truck. But I could never do that to my parents. I knew they had suffered too much already from losing one child.

Mom and Dad got more involved in church and volunteer work. A week after Mary Kaye was killed, they volunteered to take the church youth group on a campout. I had no interest in church. I'd go on Christmas for my parents' benefit, but I liked to think I was too intellectual for church to be a regular part of my life. My parents kept the angels busy by praying for my safety. They did a good job—my parents and the angels.

I still officially lived with my parents but stayed at Edward's apartment for days at a time. It was an unstable relationship with petty arguments and periodic breakups.

## Trust the Timing

During the breakups, I drove my '69 Dodge Dart the hour south to Wilmington to visit Terry and Sally or Caroline. They were all living there in the port city/college town at one time or another during the late seventies. Those were some of my wildest weekends, leaving me with not-so-fond memories of heaving over somebody's toilet at two in the morning or wondering if I should be a little more selective about who I ended up in bed with. Still, there was an element of relative safety being with my high school girlfriends who would have my back if things got too far out of control. Not to say that I was always safe, but thankfully, there was no permanent damage. The angels must have been run ragged.

I continued to work at the movies and took a break from college. There were potential adventures that I dabbled in but didn't follow through on, like accepting an offer from a lifeguard at one of the Camp Lejeune pools where I swam, thanks to Dad's retired status. This Marine Corps lifeguard volunteered to train me (for free) to *be* a lifeguard. I loved to swim, but I'd never thought of myself as someone capable of being a lifeguard, so I wouldn't have thought of it on my own. I did okay with the physically demanding tasks like treading water until my legs felt like rubber and dragging a pretending-to-be-limp body out of the pool. But there was something awkward about getting private training for this instead of being in a class. The lifeguard had not made any overt passes at me, but it just didn't feel right. It probably would have been better to have the camaraderie of classmates. After about three sessions, I just stopped showing up, which made me feel uncomfortable because I knew that wasn't right. My self-esteem floundered as my critical voice whispered something about being a quitter. Years later, I wished I'd stuck with it or found a class. I really could've been a lifeguard if I'd just hung in there.

I did complete a scuba-diving course a year or so later. The certification dive was fascinating once I got in the water. (I hadn't realized how prone I was to seasickness until then, so sitting in the rocking boat was miserable.) But being fifty feet under the water was like being on another planet with the quiet sensation of moving in slow motion as we kept an eye on the school of barracuda that didn't bother us. The instructor said we all passed our certification dive, but then he left town, and I didn't get my certification card. I just left it at that and never followed up on it.

One thing I did follow through on, at least for a while, was riding. Every now and then, I went to a stable outside of town to ride horses. There was an old cowboy there who'd gotten a good deal on two horses and offered to sell me one of them. I was living with my parents and didn't have a lot of expenses, so I jumped at the chance. It had been a childhood dream to have a horse of my own. She was a gray roan named Blue Babe and a bit high-strung. I was not all that emotionally stable either, so we didn't have the best relationship. I wasn't able to provide as much patience as she needed. Of course, I didn't hurt her, and I didn't yell at her—well, not much—but I'm sure she could feel my frustration when I was trying to put her bridle on and she'd raise her head up out of my reach. As with all relationships, we got to work on our issues. I needed to work on patience and consistency, so I had to learn to take a deep breath and calm down so that Babe would calm down and feel safe. Since I didn't have a saddle at first, I rode bareback. That made it easier for her to throw me off when she'd been out to pasture too long because I was too distracted to ride her regularly.

After a couple of months, I heard a rumor that the people I was paying to feed my horse were just tossing loaves of bread out into the pasture, so I moved her to a different stable closer to my parents' house and started spending more time with her.

The consistency of taking better care of Babe improved our relationship. I enjoyed riding around in the pasture and on wooded trails, especially after I invested in a good English saddle. We even did a little jumping over logs. It reminded me of my early adolescence when being around horses and feeling their power and energy under me offered a natural high that didn't get me into any trouble.

The people who owned the new stables were looking for someone to stay in the trailer on their property. They wanted someone to live there and keep an eye on the horses. It was a good deal, so I went for it. Then they offered to give me their headstrong St. Bernard, named Sandy.

"The only thing is, she's a little aggressive with men, so you need to watch out for that," they warned.

I'd always liked big dogs, so I said, "Sure, why not."

Sandy was very protective and came in handy when some less-than-desirable male visitor didn't want to leave.

"It's time for Sandy to go out," I'd say, getting her out of the bedroom. "Oh, did I mention she has a history of attacking men?"

That winter, I adopted two more dogs, and a barn cat slipped into my door and had a litter of kittens in my bedroom. My two-bedroom trailer was like a mini animal shelter. It was a life I would have appreciated more if I hadn't been so confused. At twenty years old, I lived in a subtle fog.

I still worked at the movie theater and had attempted a couple of other short-lived jobs on the side without much success. There were hints of depression and frustration that I was able to suppress for a while with drinking, occasional weed, and sexual encounters that were completely devoid of love—risky but thankfully, miraculously, without harm, or so I thought. The harm was below the surface—to my self-esteem. I didn't want to look at the fact that I wasn't going anywhere with my life.

One afternoon, I sat alone in my little trailer watching a movie called *The Day of the Dolphin* about two bottlenose

## Trust the Timing

dolphins who had been taught how to talk by a team of well-meaning scientists. The dolphins, Fa and Bea (Alpha and Beta), lived in a relatively natural environment and were happy dolphins. They learned to speak in high-pitched, broken English that was endearingly childlike in its simplicity. Later in the movie, Fa and Bea are kidnapped to be exploited and endangered for some evil political purpose involving explosive devices.

The ending is a tearjerker for any serious animal lover. The head scientist had of course become attached to the dolphins. They did after all call him "Pa," and they called his wife/colleague "Ma." When the dolphins miraculously made it home in the end, Pa had to tell them, for their own protection, to swim far away—out to the deep ocean—and never come back. The dolphins didn't want to go without Pa and Ma.

"Fa *love* Pa," Alpha cried.

That's when the tears started to run down my face.

Pa had to be very stern with Alpha to save him and Bea from the bad men. He told Fa and Bea they had to swim away and stay away from man forever.

To this day, I can't watch that ending without crying. I have to remind myself that *it's just a movie!* (And that the book has a happier ending.)

As I watched the movie end in the late seventies, the tears turned into sobs. Long, hard sobs like I had never cried before—sobs not only for my lost self but also for my lost sister and all the grief I'd been covering up for two years since she died. We were just starting to feel glimmers of friendship when she was killed.

The movie shook me up and out of complacency as if a veil had been lifted: *I had forgotten all about saving the whales! I was supposed to be doing something important with my life!*

I was ashamed of how far I had drifted away from my goals. I knew I had to get back into school.

I started to think about moving back in with my parents, so I could focus on school rather than paying rent. And owning a horse was getting expensive. Besides food and boarding fees, there were vet bills and blacksmith fees. The blacksmith who came to trim Blue Babe's hooves owned American Saddlebred show horses and wanted a horse just for pleasure. He was a more experienced rider than me, and when I saw how Babe perked up with him on her back, I knew she would be okay with him.

My parents graciously let me bring Sandy and a couple of the cats back home with me. I found homes for the rest. Sandy adored my dad. Not only did she show no hint of aggression toward him, she loved for him to scratch her ears and sought him out as an alpha male she could trust. As for me, I was back in a safe harbor with a sturdy platform from which I could grow. It was time to get serious about school again.

## 6

## *David*

# Fast Cars and Close Calls
(1973–1976)

The summer of '73 brought new opportunities. I was working too much, but the goal was to buy a car. I paid my boss, Polardi, $300 for a red-and-white 1966 VW bus. I figured it would be good for hauling stuff. The "Iron-Sided Shack Wagon," my grandfather called it, "a party on wheels." The bus was bone-chilling cold in the winter, and it wouldn't get past sixty-five miles per hour going downhill with a tailwind, but it didn't matter because I had freedom! It was roomy enough for a bunch of guys to pile in and go cruising around Hooterville. Every now and then, we'd go out to Barn Island to party in the empty parking lot near the boat ramp. But mostly, I just burned gas to avoid being at home. Every spare minute was spent on the road.

During that summer, I had the first recollection of JoAnne I'd had in a while. I wondered if the Iron-Sided Shack Wagon would make it to North Carolina. It would be nice to see her. I wondered if she was doing okay. I mentioned it once to my mother and was told, "Why do you want to do that? You can't drive that far." Again, I listened.

Then it was back to school in the fall for my senior year. I still had a math class to retake because of the move, so I took geometry and algebra 2 at the same time. I was becoming more rebellious in some ways and more conforming in others. My hair had grown down to my shoulders since my father had given up that fight. I spent a lot of time in my room trying to stay under his radar and to avoid negative comments. I hated school, but I was constantly being told I had to go to school to get a good job. So I focused on surviving my senior year and getting school over with while I worked afternoons and weekends at the gas station. At work, I was punctual and trained new staff. At school, I did the bare minimum and rarely participated in class discussions except for history class when we read *TIME* magazine and talked about current events. I was mostly interested in real stuff like the unfolding of Watergate and the tornado outbreak in Ohio that wrapped a Dodge van around a telephone pole.

One of the people who helped me make it to graduation was Mr. Lonsway. He'd been a science teacher until he was drafted and deployed to Vietnam where he served as a journalist. In his late twenties, he returned to the states and became a guidance counselor. He often pulled me into his office to encourage or to challenge me.

# Trust the Timing

"Hey, you're screwin' up. What's goin' on?"

"What do you mean?"

"Your grades aren't that good. Something's going on. You're smarter than that."

"I'm just not that into school." I shrugged.

I never talked to Mr. Lonsway about anything going on at home. Experience had taught me that the consequences of talking about my home life could be severe. When I was ten years old, my father found out I had told something about our family to someone outside the family. I don't recall what I told; it might have been something minor. But what I remember clearly is my father in my face screaming, "YOU DON'T TELL ANYBODY WHAT HAPPENS IN THIS HOUSE!" Telling wasn't worth my father's wrath. So whenever anyone asked me how things were going at home, I said, "okay."

It was Mr. Lonsway who had passed me in the hallway my junior year and told me about the job at the gas station. He must have been looking out for me. He was one of the few people who had confidence in me. Maybe that's why I invited him to the Deep Purple concert.

I got four tickets to go to New Haven to see Deep Purple in April of my senior year. I'd asked a couple of friends and then, on a whim, asked Mr. Lonsway. I figured he'd probably say no. He said he'd get back to me. The next day, I stopped by his office on my way to class.

"So, you goin'?"

"Yeah, I'll go to the concert."

## A Memoir of Finding Love Again

"Cool!"

We all met at the school and left at five thirty. Out of respect, we let Mr. Lonsway ride shotgun. On the way to the concert, he was like one of the guys, joking and laughing. The New Haven Coliseum was designed as a hockey arena, so the steps were steep. We climbed to our seats behind the stage, close to the speakers. It was one of my first major rock concerts, and even from behind, it was a good show with lots of energy. A joint came my way, but I waved it off. I was there to enjoy the show. Mr. Lonsway waved it off, too, as expected.

On the ride home, we all laughed and talked about the concert and about our ears ringing. We had to talk loud anyway to be heard above the radio, which had to be loud to be heard above the engine noise of the Shack Wagon. So after a while we just listened to the radio. It was after midnight when we dropped Mr. Lonsway off at the school where he'd left his car. He said he liked the show and thanked me for inviting him. In later years, I realized it was the least I could do for all of his encouragement.

A couple of weeks after the concert, the motor in the Shack Wagon burned up. I took it apart on a Saturday and replaced a piston, cylinder, and rings over the next few days. It felt good to be able to fix my own vehicle, thanks to what I'd learned working at the gas station. I'd even gotten my boss to show me how to work the winch on the tow truck, which led to me driving the wrecker

## Trust the Timing

in the last half of my senior year. I'd get called up in the middle of the night, sometimes two or three times a week in the winter. Mom was not happy with this.

"Why can't Polardi go out on those friggin' wrecker calls himself, instead of sending my son out in this weather?"

I didn't mind it. The sense of accomplishment I felt at being able to pull cars out of ditches, out of trees, or out of other cars—not to mention the extra money—made up for the inconvenience of getting up in the middle of the night.

By the skin of my teeth, I finally graduated high school on June 19, 1974, in the half of the class that made the top class possible. It was a huge relief. *Now I can really go to work,* I thought. During the summer after graduation, I worked two and three jobs to stay busy and make money to buy another car. My brother had wrecked the Shack Wagon in a game of chicken, fortunately without permanent damage except to my vehicle.

It was in October of '74 that I bought "The Monster." It was a black '69 Chevelle with a 396 cubic-inch motor, a four-speed transmission, and 3.08 gears in the rear. It wasn't fast off the line, and I started out pretty mellow for the first week or so. But the tachometer showed there were a lot of RPMs left to go in that engine. One quiet weekday afternoon, I decided it was time for a speed test on I-95. As soon as I passed under the Boom Bridge Road overpass, I had a clear run. I dropped into third gear and mashed the accelerator to the floor. Every nerve in my body became more alive. I passed cars going half my speed in under two seconds. I'd never gone that fast before. I was hooked.

I'd had the Chevelle for a few weeks when I thought of taking Mom for a ride, hoping to share the excitement. I didn't have a girlfriend at the time. I'd dated here and there but nothing long term. I was too focused on work to have a steady girlfriend. Mom had been working at the bank all week. I figured she could use some fun. We drove out to Route 184 nice and easy. I wound out the RPMs slowly before shifting, so she wouldn't feel the acceleration right away.

Going down Pious Hill, Mom asked, "How fast are we going?"

I didn't say anything, continuing to accelerate as I noticed the needle just passing 120 miles per hour.

"Slow down! How fast are we going?" Mom yelled.

I looked at the speedometer. "140," I said.

"Stop this car! Stop this car now! Slow this car down right now!"

Mom was some kinda mad. So I backed off the accelerator.

"Take me home!" she demanded with fire coming out of her eyes. She was pretty upset with me but calmed down by the time we got to the traffic circle a mile and a half down the road.

"That was cool, huh?" I grinned.

## Trust the Timing

"Don't you *ever* drive that fast again!"

Several months later, Mom would enjoy bragging to my brother's hot-rod friends about how fast she had been going down Pious Hill.

"You boys ain't got nothin' on me," she'd say. "I've been 140 miles an hour on that road." Then, being the parent, she made it clear that it was a foolish endeavor and that we should always drive the speed limit.

Driving the Chevelle was my favorite pastime. My job at the gas station paid for gas, parts, and car insurance. I stayed busy running the gas pumps and doing small repairs on cars and tires. One day, when I was working too fast and not paying attention, I shoved a tire reamer through the webbing between my left thumb and forefinger and spent a few days in the hospital on antibiotics. Being out on workers' comp for a couple of weeks bored me nuts, so I drove by Brad's house to find him working outside. We had been friends since fourth grade, but I hadn't seen him in a year or more.

I got out, and we talked for a while about him getting ready to go in the Army. I'd thought about going into the Air Force and flying jets but figured I wasn't smart enough. Wanting to shake those thoughts, I said, "Hey, you want to go for a ride?"

We set out driving on a secondary road, and I said the most dangerous words to ever be uttered: "Watch *this*."

I mashed the accelerator, and before long we were at top speed. We traveled the length of a football field

## A Memoir of Finding Love Again

in just over one second. As we rounded a curve, we saw the intersection about a quarter mile away. A car was pulling out to cross our path while a pickup truck was coming the other way. Disaster was imminent! I tried the brakes and nothing. The vacuum was gone because the carburetor was so far open. I downshifted to slow down to seventy-five miles per hour and somehow threaded my car between the two vehicles.

I pulled into the Shell station. We sat there for a minute not saying anything, feeling our heartbeats.

"Whoa. We can't do that anymore," I said. We both realized we should be dead—not just us but Ruthie, the newspaper lady, and her dad who were in her car and the town's fire chief in his pickup truck.

It was then that I had my first realization that there is a higher power, and we are all part of a plan. I knew right then that there was a reason I was spared. I didn't know why or what it would be, but I knew.

Six weeks later, on a night right before Christmas, a guy I worked with at the gas station died on the same road, a half-mile west of Pious Hill. He hit the embankment driving far too fast.

It could have been me.

It was a good thing that the engine of the Chevelle failed after my brother took it out for a spin and spun a bearing, which meant I could no longer go that fast. I think he did me a favor. I didn't tell Mom about the close call at the bottom of Pious Hill until many years later when she was reminiscing about her wild ride. When I told her about my narrow escape with Brad, she said she hated that car more than I'd ever know.

I slowed down a lot after the Pious Hill incident and never got in any big trouble, though in later years, Mom enjoyed reminding me of the time I called her to pick me up from a party in the summer after graduation. I didn't drink often, so I didn't have much tolerance. I have no memory of this incident, but as Mom tells it, she brought me home and snuck me upstairs. I was laughing and talking loud in the shower while my brother mocked me with an evangelical litany about the evils of alcohol—a parody of the religious TV shows my father watched on Sundays. Mom tried to shush us both. She must have been successful because my father didn't hear us from his throne in the living room that night. If he had, I would have remembered.

# 7

## *JoAnne*

# It's So Easy to Fall in Love
### (1977–1989)

Once I got serious about school, the small community college turned out to be a good fit. With the diversity of nontraditional students from a variety of backgrounds—old, young, black, white, mostly middle-class people—it was easy to make friends. I worked on the student newspaper and joined the student government. My basic core classes were easy, and I loved biology. Being a big fish in a little pond worked wonders for my self-esteem. Everything was fine until trigonometry.

My instructors for trig and chemistry were intellectual men who lectured with little expression or interaction. It felt like pieces were missing, like there was another math class I had forgotten to take after algebra 2. I managed to get a D in trig, but that wouldn't transfer to a university. When I started getting lost in chemistry, I dropped the class so it wouldn't hurt my grade point average. (I found out later the instructor started curving test scores after I dropped.) I could have gotten a tutor, but that

## Trust the Timing

was a foreign idea to me. I thought I should be smart enough not to need a tutor. There would be more math and science ahead if I was going to major in biology. The thought of calculus and physics made my stomach tense.

I'd always been good in art and languages but valued science more. (Maybe it was all those *Star Trek* episodes that helped me through puberty.) Out of curiosity, I took a psychology class and found it *"fascinating,"* as Spock might say. It was a science I could easily make A's in. And wasn't the scientist in *The Day of the Dolphin* a psychologist? Maybe biology wasn't the only field where I could make a difference.

I didn't know it consciously, but psychology was what I *needed* to study. It would ultimately put me in work settings that forced me to grow—not just intellectually but emotionally. It would give me the tools I needed to work on me in a way that biology could not have done. Studying psychology would push me along on the endless journey of my own healing.

Once I changed my major, I became more comfortable at the community college. My parents didn't mind me living with them while I was in school, and grant money paid for my tuition and books. I was so comfortable I didn't want to leave, so I stayed for a third year, taking electives I thought would be interesting. Along with more psychology, I took sociology, journalism, music, and even acting.

Acting was something new for me. Being an introvert,

## A Memoir of Finding Love Again

I was uncomfortable about getting up in front of people and saying lines. But improvising got to be fun once I learned to let go, to let myself be silly—even dramatic—and not just live inside my own head. It was so much fun being spontaneous with a creative bunch of people that I ended up taking all three levels of acting in my third year. My confidence grew steadily.

In acting class, I met Brian, a tall, good-natured guy with a ponytail that reached halfway down his back. He was full of imagination and liked to experiment with goofy accents during class. One day in January, Brian asked me if I was going to a play in the community for extra credit.

"Yeah, I was thinking about it," I said.

"Would you mind giving me a ride?"

"Sure. I wouldn't mind." I thought he was cute. And he was tall.

After the play, we went to the neighborhood tavern and had a beer, maybe two, and discovered we both liked science fiction and art. Brian had both a fondness and talent for drawing heroic Amazonian women with voluptuous bodies not unlike my own, though exaggerated to fantastic proportions. An hourglass figure is one thing, but how many small-waisted women can there be, with breasts the size of honeydews, fighting bad guys in between trips to the chiropractor for their back problems? But knowing that he liked big women encouraged me.

## Trust the Timing

Our winter class project was *A Midsummer Night's Dream*. Brian and I were cast as two of the four lovers confused by a magic spell. Everyone in our group got to be good friends by rehearsing together outside of class. We'd practice our lines in the cafeteria, or we'd all go over to Eddy Cowalsky's house and rehearse in his parents' rec room. The four of us playing the lovers were nervous during the love scenes, as none of us had done this sort of thing before. Brian's character was only briefly enamored of mine, but when he professed his love to me with a light touch on my arm during rehearsal, in Shakespearean lingo, my skin tingled, and I couldn't remember my lines! That didn't happen with my "true" onstage lover. I had no trouble remembering my lines with the other guy, even when he kissed me as the script directed. It was fun, but there were no butterflies. When Brian came close to me and looked in my eyes, I felt the magic of a chemical attraction that extended beyond the stage.

I found myself drawn to Brian's sense of humor, which was sometimes dry, sometimes playful. He was kind, like a gentle giant. One day when we were hanging out at his parents' house, his mother spotted a spider crawling up the wall in the living room.

"Brian, get that spider," she urged. "The flyswatter's in the kitchen!"

But instead of the flyswatter, Brian got a cup and guided the spider into it. Then he took the little spider outside and released it among the hydrangea bushes.

"Do you always do that with spiders?" I asked.

"Yes," he said, then added in his Russian accent, "Dere's no need to keel dem. Dey have da right to live, jus' like us."

That pretty much did it. Even though he didn't claim to love animals like I did, he had enough compassion to take the spider outside instead of killing it. I knew I would be safe with Brian.

In the early spring, we both auditioned for the community-college production of *Alice in Wonderland*. It was based on a 1970's off-Broadway version and was described as how a small group of children confined to a padded cell would recreate the story of Alice. We each played multiple parts. I played the haughty Red Queen and the zany White Queen—both confidence-building roles. Brian was brilliant romping around the stage in patched overalls that showed off the muscles in his arms and chest. Performing outside on spring evenings, dancing and twirling with Alice in Wonderland, Brian and I fell in love.

It was a carefree time full of the impulsiveness of invincible youth. One night at the tavern, we were sitting around with friends, and the conversation meandered into the subject of marriage.

I don't remember who asked the question, "Do you want to get married?"—me or Brian. It might have been something I blurted out since this was one of the few

## Trust the Timing

times in my life I was good at being spontaneous. I do remember that the question was asked in the same way one would ask, "Do you want to order a pizza?"

The response was probably something profound like, "Okay. Let's do it!" followed by confident smiles and the clinking of beer mugs.

Brian and I got married in August of 1980 and looked forward to a bright future of happily ever after. For our honeymoon, we bought five pounds of shrimp and took his parents' pop-up camper to the beach for the weekend. A week later, we moved to a one-bedroom apartment in historic downtown Wilmington, an hour away, so I could finish college at the university. When cold weather came, we discovered a hole in the loaf of bread we'd put on top of the refrigerator. We had mice. Or maybe they were small rats. I don't know. Thankfully, Brian accepted the duty of trapping them the old-fashioned way, something I couldn't bear to be a part of. That spring we heard something mewing and discovered a tiny kitten under the house. The landlady had made it clear she didn't want any pets in the house, and it wouldn't have surprised me if she'd had the rest of the family picked up by animal control. Still, we adopted the remaining little one and named her Ramble. Fortunately, the house ended up being sold to a man who was more accepting of pets. We didn't see any more rodents after that.

In my senior year, I volunteered a few hours a week

at the local crisis hotline. That position grew into my first full-time grown-up job after I graduated with a psychology degree. Working the phones at the crisis line, I never knew who was going to call or when. People called about all kinds of things—domestic violence, drugs, loneliness, eviction, and problem pregnancies. The variety made it an interesting job, and it was rewarding to help people explore more options than they thought they had or offer a new possibility. In addition to the crisis line, we had a shelter for teenagers on-site for runaways or kids who had been abused. Some of these kids stirred up the beginnings of my maternal instinct. It's hard not to feel maternal when you're taking care of a sick kid with a fever or debunking obvious misconceptions about how to prevent pregnancy with a sexually active, fourteen-year-old girl who comes in past curfew. I learned a lot in the three years I worked there and might have stayed with that job longer, but the overnight shifts did not fit with our desire to start a family. When the opportunity presented itself, I moved up to a job as substance abuse counselor with almost normal hours.

The new job was more challenging. My listening and problem-solving skills were good, and I had a clear understanding of behavior modification, but my supervisor kept urging me, "You've got to be more *confrontive.*" Back in the early eighties, direct confrontation was still a primary tool in the substance abuse field, though it was *not* taught in college. To be more "confrontive," I had to work on my self-esteem and confidence issues.

A superficial sense of confidence came from smoking cigarettes. In those days, smoking in counseling sessions was commonplace. Since most of my clients (and a lot of coworkers) smoked, it was a way of joining with a client, even though we knew it wasn't healthy. Clients giving up drugs or drinking rarely want to tackle smoking at the same time. "I've got to have *some* kind of vice," they say. And who was I to encourage them to quit cigarettes when I still smoked?

I'd quit smoking lots of times. Back when I lived in the trailer at the stables, I threw away my cigarettes regularly and fished them out of the trash fifteen minutes later. Then, after smoking one, I broke them all in half and threw them away again. Once I taped a broken cigarette back together but gagged when I got to the taped part. I held the rest of the pack under the kitchen faucet, and, a couple of hours later, discovered that wet cigarettes tend to fall apart when you try to dry them out in the oven. So I bought another pack.

When I worked at the crisis hotline, I quit smoking for several months, but noticing that a couple of coworkers could smoke occasionally, I thought I could do that too. I rationalized that the stress of working at a crisis line should entitle me to smoke at least when I was working. For a while I only bummed cigarettes and only smoked at work. I made sure I had breath mints or gum before

I went home. I had no reason to hide my smoking from Brian except for the denial that I'd relapsed. And shame about the relapse. And shame about the denial. That's addiction for ya.

One day, Brian showed up at my job to surprise me and caught me smoking at the crisis line desk as I was writing up my notes from the last call.

"So how long have you been smoking?" he asked.

"Maybe a month. And *only at work*," I explained. "It's a stressful job."

He just shook his head and walked out without saying much more.

Brian didn't smoke cigarettes, though he did enjoy his beer. I think his disappointment wasn't so much about me risking my health as it was about me hiding my smoking from him. I'd never been dishonest about anything with him before. When it came to cigarettes, I was a true addict. I couldn't smoke even a little without it creeping up on me. After I got caught, I relapsed back to a pack a day.

As a substance abuse counselor, I learned more about addiction and recovery, including how addicting cigarettes are. If you use a drug twenty times a day, you're going to have a lot of triggers. Though cigarette warnings had increased, there wasn't much help available for quitting, not like there was for other addictions. That continues to be true, even though I've been told by heroin addicts that quitting cigarettes is harder than quitting heroin.

## Trust the Timing

Smoking gave me horrible headaches behind my eyes and a cough that lingered for weeks after every cold. I was tired of gasping for air when I went up a few flights of stairs. Smoking never did fit with who I was. It was totally incongruent with my love for nature and efforts to become a vegetarian. Plus, I wanted to quit before I got pregnant.

I decided to piece together my own program. I read everything I could find about quitting smoking, taped pictures of diseased lungs on my refrigerator, and made lists. On the benefits list, I wrote that I'd save thirty dollars a month and made a plan to put one dollar (that's what a pack cost back in the early eighties) into a jar for every day I didn't smoke. Maybe I'd buy myself one of the earthy tapestries I'd seen hanging in a shop downtown.

I made a long list of coping strategies, including everything from taking a shower to screaming into a pillow. It was hard, the hardest thing I'd ever done (I hadn't raised teenagers yet), but once I committed to do *"whatever it takes,"* my plan worked. After sixty days, I bought myself the big brown-and-white tapestry with the Native American designs and hung it in the living room.

Another addiction I wanted to reign in before I got pregnant was compulsive overeating. I'd been slightly overweight as a child yet got in good shape with all the activity in junior high and high school and my first years in college. But after I got married, I gained forty pounds.

## A Memoir of Finding Love Again

Brian and I both liked to eat and reinforced each other's indulgences, especially early in the marriage when we were still immortal.

When I worked at the crisis line, one of the big donut chains donated a trash bag full of donuts every week, and I'd grab one mindlessly when I walked through the kitchen. Being tall, I'd always been able to carry a lot of weight. (Mom used to say I was big-boned.) But the denial started to crumble when someone asked me when my baby was due, and I wasn't pregnant yet.

We didn't have a bathroom scale at home, so I was shocked when I visited my parents and their scale had the nerve to tell me I weighed over 220.

*How the hell did that happen?* I asked the woman in the bathroom mirror with tears in her eyes.

I promised myself to work on losing weight and managed, by sheer willpower, to lose around thirty pounds before I got pregnant.

Our son was born in 1985. We named him Isaac after Brian's grandfather. And there was Isaac Asimov, the science fiction writer, and Isaac Bashevis Singer, who inspired me with his powerful writing about vegetarianism. I was nowhere near being a perfect vegetarian. To this day, I struggle with shellfish . . . and salmon . . . and casseroles with hidden chicken, but I've believed in the cause ever since college when I read an article by a hunter who wrote that everyone opposed to hunting must be either a vegetarian or a hypocrite.

# Trust the Timing

Giving birth brought a profound biological and spiritual awakening. I had never understood why people went all gaga over babies until I had one of my own. I must have been very susceptible to the bonding hormones produced by my body. Breastfeeding, though a bit challenging at first, became fascinating once I figured out I had to *relax* for the milk to "let down." It amazed me how my body's milk production adjusted to the needs of my baby. Nature works amazingly well when we let things flow. Not to mention that breastfeeding helped keep my weight down.

The bond of protection and love I felt for my little offspring was like nothing I had ever experienced. It was the first time I knew beyond any doubt that I would be willing to protect someone with my life. I started driving the speed limit and crying over the TV news. For the first time in years, I started thinking about going back to church, but it was just a thought.

As Isaac grew, we started calling him Zack because it sounded cool. We decided Brian would stay home to take care of him when I went back to work after maternity leave. It was a logical arrangement since Brian could work on his art career from home. We were a progressive, outside-the-box little family in our historic downstairs apartment with high ceilings, tall windows, and a big front porch surrounded by azalea bushes. Life was good for the most part, though leaving my baby to go back to my job was not as easy as I thought it would be. The

## A Memoir of Finding Love Again

sentimental stirrings of parenthood, combined with the stress of my job and listening to my clients talk about God from a twelve-step perspective, all got me thinking more about church. I needed a greater source of strength. My early childhood memories of a big Catholic church in Washington, DC, whispered to me. I remembered quietly drawing pictures, using the pew for my desk, as the mystical feel of the Latin liturgy seeped into my four-year-old brain. The red, glowing candles beckoned me, and I always asked to light one so I could get a closer look. We stayed in Washington sometimes when Dad was deployed on a ship, and my mom's aunt Josephine, a devout Catholic, insisted on reading to me from the Bible every afternoon at the kitchen table. Aunt Jo was hard to understand because Parkinson's disease made her shake uncontrollably, but I knew that the Bible and prayers she recited must have been very important for her to make me sit there and listen for no less than twenty minutes.

My dad was Protestant, Moravian to be exact, and we attended both Protestant and Catholic services at base chapels when I was growing up. In my teens, I stopped going to church except on the holy days when going to church was a gift to my parents who were active in the Methodist Church. They didn't push me, but the evangelical, conservative Christian preachers they watched on TV in the late seventies turned me off in a big way. I had nightmares about them hunting me down and taking me off to a remote compound, where I had to

## Trust the Timing

pretend to go along as I planned my escape.

As an adult, I liked thinking of myself as an intellectual agnostic. Back when I was starting at the crisis hotline, my coworker, a guitar-playing hippie who probably majored in philosophy, talked with me objectively about religion. I shared with him my childhood memories of the Catholic Church and my fear of the crazy conservative Christians.

"You might like the Episcopal Church," he said. "They look and feel like Catholics, but they're more open-minded." I tucked that seed away in my "interesting but not yet relevant" file.

When Zack was about a year old, I saw a newspaper photo of the Blessing of the Animals at Good Shepherd Episcopal Church. Through my job, I'd heard about this same church having a free soup kitchen. I was curious. Maybe this was worth investigating. What did I have to lose? Though he believed in God, Brian wasn't interested in church. So I decided to go by myself.

The first thing I saw when I walked into the sanctuary of the old brick church was the stained-glass window of the Good Shepherd. The window took up most of the back wall behind the altar. The richness of the colors captivated me. Jesus and his sheep were surrounded by lush, green grapevines. His deep-red robe, glowing from the light outside, reminded me of the red candles in the Catholic church of my early childhood. Jesus looked lovingly at the lamb cradled in his arm. His expression was one of acceptance and compassion. For me, it was love at first sight.

Several members of the congregation greeted me with warm smiles and handshakes during "The Peace" in the middle of the service. Afterward, they told me how glad they were to meet me and invited me to come back. I scheduled an appointment with the pastor, Burton, who was close to my age. I wondered how he would react to my questioning of some of the conservative dogma that had kept me away from church. Would he tell me I was going to hell if I didn't believe everything in the Bible literally?

During our meeting the following Saturday, I took a chance and laid out my concerns. "I just can't believe those things about men having dominion over the women and over the earth," I told him. Burton told me about the "three-legged stool" of scripture, tradition, and reason and that the Episcopal Church used all three legs for balance. My questions were welcomed with open-minded intelligence from Burton and from others in the church who considered scripture from both spiritual and historical perspectives. The three-legged stool made sense to me. If that had not been the case, if I had heard anything about women needing to be submissive to men or the earth being here solely for the benefit of man, I would have hightailed it out of there and never looked back, no matter how nice the people were. But the acceptance, the inclusiveness, offered safety, which, in time, allowed me to overcome my fear of judgment and open up to learn about the love of Jesus.

Over the next year, I went to church more Sundays than not and continued to grow spiritually at a slow but steady rate. I took Zack with me some, and Brian went with us on the big holidays. My newfound spirituality helped me cope with the challenges of my job and life in general. I began to consider that maybe it wasn't all up to me to save the world, and maybe my self-worth didn't have to depend on how much I helped others, and maybe I needed to love others as myself, not more than myself.

It was only a beginning. My codependence was still alive and well, but I did start taking better care of myself and getting more exercise while doing my best to juggle work and family life.

When Zack was two years old, Brian got a job outside the home and worked on his art at night and on weekends. He took Zack to day care on his way to work and picked him up in the evenings. Zack wasn't happy about not staying home with his dad anymore, but taking his cuddly yellow "Big Bird" with him helped. On their way home one day, Brian and Zack found a stray puppy in the road and brought him home as a surprise. I was delighted! I'd missed having a dog in the house.

Before Zack was born, back when I started working at the crisis hotline and felt able to afford a dog, we had brought my St. Bernard, Sandy, to Wilmington. She'd stayed with my parents shortly after Brian and I got married, and I'd forgotten to keep up with her heartworm preventative, a sin I still have trouble forgiving myself for. When we brought her to live with us and took her to the vet, Sandy was heartworm positive. Her treatment included keeping her from getting excited. I expected it to work. One day when I came home from a trying forty-eight-hour shift, Sandy was happy to see me. She danced around me, wanting to play.

"I'm happy to see you too, girl!" I told her and ruffled her fur ever so gently. Then she started coughing up blood. We took her to the after-hours vet, who said Sandy would need to stay overnight. I sat with her in the kennel for about an hour and then decided to go home to get some sleep. When I called the next morning, the vet said Sandy died right after I left. He said there wasn't much we could have done and that seven years was not a bad life span for such a large breed. But to this day, I still beat myself up about leaving Sandy that night. I cried for days and kept berating myself about how I should have kept her on heartworm preventative. I should have kept her calm! I should have stayed with her at the vet. I should never have left her alone! I promised myself I would never again leave a dog who's that sick.

Even with the heartaches, a house is not a home to me without a dog, so Brian bringing home a new puppy was almost as exciting as a new baby. Brian named him Dobbs after the character played by Humphrey Bogart

# Trust the Timing

in *The Treasure of the Sierra Madre*. Dobbs could not have been more than a couple of months old. His ears were long and floppy, but his coloring looked like a German shepherd. As he grew up, he looked like a shepherd/lab mix. Zack and Dobbs got along great. I'd already taught my son to gently stroke our cat, Ramble, instead of squeezing, so that helped prepare him to be gentle with our new puppy. Dobbs kept his distance from Ramble after she swatted the rambunctious pup a couple of times.

While Dobbs was still a puppy, we bought a small house with a big, fenced-in backyard, which had always been my dream. A big house would have been okay too, but the big backyard with a fence was the priority. As Dobbs and Zack grew, they would have the run of the yard in relative safety. We had plenty of room for a garden, fires for roasting marshmallows, and Zack's birthday parties.

A couple of years after we moved into the new house, we had the first white Christmas our part of the South had seen in a very long time. In Wilmington, it came to be known as "The Blizzard of 1989." I'll always remember it as the Christmas Eve I spent in the hospital.

The pregnancy had come as a surprise because I'd been conscientious and successful with natural birth-control methods for four years. We hadn't planned to have another baby, but after we found out, we started to get excited. After the first trimester, we thought it was safe to tell Zack and to share our excitement with family, friends, and coworkers.

On the afternoon of Christmas Eve, I was sixteen weeks into the pregnancy when I felt mild cramps. I tried not to worry and decided to lie down for a while. Less than an hour later, I got up to go to the bathroom and felt the horrible, involuntary feeling of needing to push but not wanting to. I couldn't bear to look at what I felt come out of my body and yelled for Brian. He wrapped the body in a towel, which we took to the emergency room with us.

On the way there, it started snowing. Normally, this would be a cause for great excitement, but I hardly noticed the fat snowflakes. I didn't even care whether or not the snow would stick. Brian stayed at the hospital with me for an hour or so and then left to go tell Zack what had happened. Our son was with neighbors and didn't know why we had to go to the hospital so suddenly. My body didn't want to let go of the placenta, so the doctor decided to do a D&C. When I woke from the surgery, feeling groggy, they decided I would stay the night since it had turned out to be one of those big snowstorms that brought all travel to a complete halt in the South.

The next day, our neighbor with four-wheel drive brought Brian to come pick me up at the hospital. It was Christmas Day, but it didn't feel like it. Back at home, I watched Brian and Zack play in the snow with Dobbs. Usually, I'd be right in there playing with them, but I felt dazed and lethargic, only able to force an occasional smile.

I cried off and on for weeks wondering, *Why did this happen to me? What could I have done differently?* I had taken good care of myself and done everything right as far as I knew. Stress at work was the only thing I could think of that I might have handled better. I shouldn't have let the arrogance of that court-ordered argumentative client or the lack of resources for the young woman who kept relapsing get to me so much. Maybe I should have rested more.

A couple of days after Christmas, the hospital called about results of an autopsy. I don't remember if I requested an autopsy, or if they assumed we wanted it done, or maybe it was a standard procedure. I decided to go look at the body to try to get a better understanding of what had happened and maybe find some closure. I told Zack, who was four, of my plans and that Burton, our pastor from Good Shepherd, would come and stay with him since Brian had to work.

"I want to see the baby, too!" Zack declared. I hesitated, but Zack was insistent, and I agreed he could come along.

I went into the pathology lab first while Zack waited in an adjoining office. The ER doctor had told us it was a boy, but the pathologist said it was too early to be sure. The body was a few inches long. I expected the large head from pictures I'd seen in textbooks but was surprised at how thin and long the arms and legs were. The doctor showed me where the umbilical cord was wrapped tightly around the little neck multiple times. He said the fetus was otherwise normal.

It felt surreal. My mind was drawn to safe analytical questions like wondering why the baby would continue to turn in the same direction over and over to make the cord wrap like that.

There was no explanation. I just had to feel the sadness.

I still wasn't sure if it was a good idea to let Zack come in. Burton said that his reaction would depend a lot on how I handled things. I went to ask my son if he was sure he wanted to see the baby. He was sure, so Burton brought Zack in to see the baby.

My son had lots of questions about the autopsy cuts that had been made on the torso. The doctor was probably not used to children being involved in this kind of viewing. His hand shook slightly as he took it upon himself to put the little body back in the Styrofoam container.

"Why is he putting our baby in a cup?" Zack asked.

I thought briefly about bringing the body home and having a burial in the yard beside the house like we'd done with baby birds that didn't survive, but that felt like too much to think about right then.

"The doctor is going to take care of the body," I told him. "The baby's soul is safe in heaven."

## Trust the Timing

Zack accepted that answer. It made sense to him. Later, he came up with the idea that "maybe that soul wasn't ready to be born yet."

I was amazed that Zack could come up with that possibility. It was a comforting thought. It helped heal the little hole in my heart that got smaller with time but never closed completely.

8

*David*

# New Responsibilities
(1975–1995)

After the Chevelle died, I was kind of aimless for a while. The economy had tanked, and I was laid off from the gas station. I worked at menial jobs and collected unemployment for a few months, just existing, trying not to spend too much time at home and escaping to friends' houses sometimes for days.

Mobility is important when you don't want to be at home, so cars still took up most of my free time. I went back to driving VWs and then had a Vega. It was a Band-Aid car; I constantly had to replace parts and wires. The Vega was fun, though, when I could get it to backfire or leave a cloud of smoke behind. It was a good thing I knew how to work on cars. I worked at an auto-parts store making deliveries and stocking inventory for about six months until they laid me off. Then I worked part time at two gas stations for a few months until I got a full-time job doing mechanic work at a truck stop down the street from my parents' house. At the truck stop, I adjusted

## Trust the Timing

brakes, learned to drive a tractor trailer, and changed a lot of tires. Once I got a whole case of frozen bagels as a tip for changing a tire. Then in 1976, I stopped by to see Polardi at the gas station. His business had picked back up, and he offered me a better deal than the truck stop. Polardi was always easy to get along with, but I knew it wasn't what I wanted to do for the rest of my life.

All this time, I'd been applying for a job with a large factory. The goal was a career with benefits. For the first six months, I went every week to the personnel office. Then I went once a month. The ladies in the office knew me by sight.

"I'm just here to follow up on my application," I'd say cheerfully.

"We don't have anything yet," they'd reply.

"Okay, thanks."

Then finally, after eighteen months, I got a phone call to come in for an interview. After the interview, they took me and four other candidates around a building full of steel pipes and machinery.

"There's a lot of pipes here," I said. "Am I going to have to learn where all these pipes go?"

"It takes time, but yes. You won't have a problem with it," the foreman said.

I was the only one who asked questions. They called me back about a week later and offered me a job as a technician. I was excited and thought I was in the big time. For years, all I had been taught by my parents, teachers, and society in general was to "go to school, get a good job, and become a middle-class American." I was on my way!

On my new job, I learned about pipes, conduits, industrial equipment, and machinery along with chemical processes. I liked to ask questions about how things worked. Some supervisors liked to answer questions. Some didn't. The hardest part of the job was working rotating shifts—a culture shock for someone young and single. The need to make sleep a priority during the day, so I could work the night shifts, tested my maturity. Sometimes I missed work, especially in that first year.

Most of my absences were for legitimate reasons, like getting sick after being told to hose down a sidewalk when it was twenty degrees outside and my pants froze. My health was not helped by the fact I'd been smoking cigarettes since eleventh grade, which messed up my sinuses and gave me terrible headaches. I smoked off and on for years with episodes of quitting followed by relapses, which happened mostly in bars where I'd be influenced by peers and beers. The smoking made my sinus problems worse and led to chronic bronchitis.

After I got health insurance to go to the doctor, he looked in my nose and said, "Oh, no. You've got a lot of polyps up there." So I had surgery on my sinuses, which was like a D&C on my face, leaving me with so little control over my nasal secretions that my nostrils had to be packed with gauze for a week. For two weeks after that, sneezing was a new adventure in pain. I quit smoking for a few months after the surgery but then went back to smoking half a pack a day off and on until I was almost thirty and tired of bronchitis and feeling like crap. That's when I finally made a commitment to quit smoking for good.

A couple of the absences in my early career were not so legitimate. I still needed discipline that would come from new responsibilities. About six months after starting at the factory, I met a woman through a mutual friend. Even though she was thirteen years older than me, Donna had a carefree spirit that I had never experienced before. She had five kids and her own apartment. I lived with my parents in a house where I still walked on eggshells much of the time, which wasn't easy with rebellion percolating inside me. Donna provided a welcome escape. And she made the meanest mac and cheese I'd ever tasted. We dated for a few months and got married. It seemed like a good idea at the time.

At the age of twenty, I acquired what my coworkers called a "ready-made family" and became the sole income earner for the household, providing food, clothing, and shelter to a family of seven plus two dogs. This greatly strengthened my commitment to working at the factory. Having been brought up to accept responsibility fostered the belief that I needed to work harder. So, I started cutting wood where people wanted to clear lots, which helped us save on heating expenses, and I could sell some of the wood. That winter I also plowed snow and worked overtime at the factory as much as I could.

Donna's kids ranged from four to fourteen years old. The older kids weren't happy about their mother marrying someone barely out of his teens with a different perspective from what they were brought up with. The family I grew up in, with two brothers and an unpredictable father, did not allow for much drama, at least not from the offspring. In my family of origin, expressing my feelings was discouraged, to put it nicely, so I was not in any way prepared for my new role in this family where everyone was free to express an opinion.

Arguments about whose turn it was to wash dishes and me being asked "couldn't you go back to work?" either sent me to bed early or outside to bond with the dog.

"We wish you never came here!" announced one of the younger children.

"He doesn't mean that," Donna assured me. "He's just repeating what he hears."

"I know that," I said. I felt deflated but shook it off and moved on.

Things got better with time. During the summer, I'd take the boys crabbing and fishing at the beach. I taught them how to catch blue crabs for dinner and how to throw a line into the surf. The rule was that if you brought it home, you had to clean it and eat it. We'd catch porgies, sea robin, dogfish, skate, and striper. Most of them we

## Trust the Timing

threw back. We'd stay out until it was too dark to see or until the sand fleas and mosquitoes chased us home.

In later years, I took each of the boys to concerts with me. I started out taking Paul when he was seventeen and when I could get the time off. We went to see Rush, Kansas, and other bands at the civic center. It was a good way to find common ground as we talked about the show and the music. Alex was a few years younger than Paul, so he had to wait. When Alex was thirteen, he wanted to go see Ratt and Poison. I think Mötley Crüe was playing with them too.

"No, you're too young to go without a responsible adult," I told him.

"What if I buy you a ticket?"

"Well, that's different. Let me think about it."

Alex bought both of our tickets with money from his paper routes. The Ratt/Poison concert had a younger crowd, and in my early thirties, I felt like a senior citizen. But the music was alright, and the band played hard. It was good to watch Alex enjoying himself.

The easiest relationship in our family was offered by "Winnie the Wonder Dog," who adopted me as her person right off the bat. She was just a puppy when I moved in, so we were both new to the family. All she wanted was to be my buddy. She was a basset hound mix with especially long ears. When she ate, some of her food ended up on her ears, and after a few months, she'd chewed the ends of her ears ragged.

## A Memoir of Finding Love Again

Winnie loved to ride in the truck with me. In warm weather, she'd sit on my lap with her head out the window and her ears flapping in the breeze. Other times, she'd stretch out on the seat with her head in my lap, happy to be riding with her person.

In August of 1978, one year into our marriage, Donna and I drove to Florida for a vacation without the kids. Driving through North Carolina, I mentioned the desire to go through Jacksonville. I wondered what had changed physically about the place, and I thought about JoAnne. I wondered if she was okay and if she was happy. But Donna said we didn't have time to go to Jacksonville. She wanted to see her friends in Daytona Beach.

The seven-day vacation, unplanned with no reservations, was a nightmare for me. Just winging it, not knowing where we were going to stay, was not the kind of risk I liked to take. We went to a couple of beaches, stayed in cheap motels, and did the tourist stuff. Then we spent one day at Disney's Magic Kingdom. With the temperature in the mid-nineties, I didn't like standing in line for rides I considered childish. The Hall of Presidents was intriguing, and the light parade at night was kind of nice, but overall I wasn't too fond of that vacation experience. A couple of hours into our return trip, we had unexpected car repairs on the front shocks, and I was thankful to still have some money left. The next day, we hit New York City traffic at four o'clock in the afternoon.

It was such a relief to finally get home that for the

next seventeen years, I would not go on another family vacation except for the occasional weekend in New Hampshire, where I could relax, unwind, and cut wood to pay for the campground.

After the trip to Florida, I continued working hard to provide for my family so they might have a few extras. I put on two weddings, resolved countless financial challenges, and maintained the household. But there was a void in my inner core. I longed for things that had always been lacking in my life, like consistency. With Donna, I never knew what to expect. I never felt good enough. Feelings of confusion and inadequacy had been part of my life since childhood, so they were easily triggered.

In the midst of my growing sense of emptiness, I helped my mom as much as I could in her own search for consistency and self-worth. Mom had made a promise to herself to leave my father before her forty-second birthday. In 1977, she summoned the courage to keep that promise. For the first few weeks after her separation, Mom lived in the apartment upstairs from us, so we got to see each other at dinner or breakfast. Later, I helped her get her own apartment nearby, and she managed to support herself by working at the bank. Every weekend, to lift her spirits, Grampa brought her a plastic bag full of spare change he'd collected. Mom was making good progress and developing a new support system. I felt proud of her independence.

## A Memoir of Finding Love Again

I'd watched my mother pinch pennies most of my life, so it was hard for me to understand my free-spirited wife's spending habits. My check from the factory adequately covered the basics, but it was never enough to cover all the extras. Figuring out ways to meet the needs and wants of my family of seven was constantly on my mind.

In 1979, I purchased a used four-wheel drive pickup truck with a snowplow, which allowed me to take advantage of the winter weather and make money plowing snow and hauling firewood. In the spring, I planted a garden.

Working in the garden and making compost gave me something to do at home. I made a compost tumbler out of used wood, constructing the box in one morning and the stand the next. Within a couple of months, the tumbler made dark, rich compost from our kitchen scraps, leaves, and lawn clippings, which I used as a soil amendment for the garden. It was a traditional garden, about thirty by thirty feet, where I grew beans, tomatoes, yellow squash, zucchini, peppers, and watermelon.

One year, I planted dark-green Sugar Baby watermelons, but just as they were getting ripe, they disappeared. All that was left was a small yellow spot on the grass. I guess somebody enjoyed them. I did manage to keep one, and it was the tastiest watermelon I ever had.

In 1983, money was still tight. My father claimed

## Trust the Timing

to be making a lot of money repairing appliances, and I knew that was something I'd be good at. But he had refused to teach me about appliance repair, no matter how many questions I asked him in my early twenties. Nevertheless, at age twenty-six, needing more money to support a large family, I swallowed my pride and showed up at his house one morning on my day off.

"What are you doing here so early?" he asked.

"I'm gonna learn appliances today."

He grumbled a little but didn't say no this time.

My father taught me a few things like how to change a belt on a washer, how to take a dryer apart, and how to evaluate a compressor. I learned the rest on my own, looking over his shoulder, staying at arm's length in case he got frustrated and started swinging tools. Somebody from work had an old washing machine to get rid of and asked me if I wanted it. I put a new roller assembly on it, replaced the belts and two hoses, cleaned it up, and sold it for $150, making $125 profit for a half hour of work. I was off and running!

In order to do the appliance work during the day, I transferred to an evening shift at the factory, where I became a pipefitter/welder, with a minor in sheet metal and millwright work. At one point, I was even wiring motors. I worked at the factory an average of fifty hours a week and with my father on appliances about thirty hours a week.

Selling reconditioned appliances with my father was

tolerable for a while. I had the truck for pickups and deliveries. He had more time to make the repairs. But we didn't always agree on the best way to make those repairs. He tended to want to save money with used parts. I preferred to buy new belts and rollers. He scheduled jobs for me at random times, regardless of my schedule at the factory. When I told him I was working, he'd rage about me being a no-good such and such and how I was screwing up his business. That's when I started to dread the appliance work.

In December of 1987, I saw an article in the local paper about a need for volunteer firefighters to work the day shift. This was something I had always wanted to do, but my father discouraged the idea when I was growing up. He'd been a volunteer firefighter for a couple of years in the mid-sixties. After he stopped going, every time the siren went off, he'd make some negative comment about those "gung ho volunteer firefighters." I guess they had a falling out.

Since I worked an evening shift at the factory, I'd be available during the day, except that I was also trying to open a video store to make money for the appliance business. I thought about it for a while. Then one day I was putting up shelves in the store to get ready for the opening and heard the siren go off. I decided to go see if I could help out. It was less than a mile up the hill.

I got to the station as the volunteers were assembling. I knew most of them.

## Trust the Timing

"Do you guys need some help?"

"Get in the truck," they said.

I got in the back of the rescue truck, feeling excited and scared at the same time. I was basically just a ride-along, because I didn't know what to do, but I filled out an application when we got back to the station.

When my father found out, he just didn't get it.

"You've got better things to do with your time than to be up there with those people," he chastised. "You should be doing something different."

"This is want I want to do," I declared. My belief in my dreams was more important than my father's old grudges. For me, it was an opportunity to help people in need, something I had always believed in, and a way to give back to the community.

My training started with weekend classes once a month, but back then, you got to start volunteering immediately. It was a bit unnerving at first because at thirty-one, I was several years older than most of the people in training. I asked a lot of questions and attracted good mentors who took time to give good answers. Bruce, whom I'd known since I was five years old back in the old neighborhood, taught me so much on rescue techniques that it was worth getting up early to have coffee with him. I'd go to the firehouse around eight in the morning when I was on second shift at the plant, and Bruce would explain all the hows and whys of disentangling people from inanimate objects. In 1988, I passed the state certification tests to

## A Memoir of Finding Love Again

become a Firefighter 1.

One summer night after I'd finished basic training, we were called to a structure fire at a restaurant. The place had closed hours earlier, so no one was in danger. I'd already been on many fires by that time and felt exhilarated. The crew I was working with had just pulled off to the side of the building in full turnout gear, and we had to get our vitals taken. It was a routine part of every fire to get checked out by the person assigned to medical monitoring.

"You're a little high," I was informed by Joe, who was taking my blood pressure.

"What's a little high?" I was irritated.

"It's 146 over 90. It's too high. You're going to have to sit down and take a rest. I can't let you go back out there."

That spun me up higher. I responded with a few obscenities because I wanted to be back out there tearing things apart.

I loved breaking things with purpose. It wasn't just hack and slash. There were systems and methods to follow. I liked using my mind to figure out the puzzle in reverse and using my physical strength to vent frustrations constructively. It was a good workout. But for the rest of that call, I was only allowed to do light duty.

Getting pulled off the job was a wake-up call. I wanted to make sure it never happened again. I knew I had put on some weight, and it was time to get back into shape. So I started eating only what I needed to survive and started taking the stairs more. I lost thirty pounds in a matter of months, and people were asking if I was okay. I could move around better, and my blood pressure came down some, but I was still a workaholic, always pushing myself to do better.

A career transfer from production to maintenance at the factory provided a steady shift, more job satisfaction, and a better work environment, but a little less money at first. The salary decrease and being a volunteer at the fire department were not well received at home.

"What are we supposed to do for money?" Donna demanded.

"I guess you're just going to have to learn to budget better," I said.

"So we're *all* going to have to suffer for your stupid whims? Why can't you be like everybody else?"

"Because I'm not like everybody else."

Donna huffed and stormed out of the room. I knew I was in for a night of the silent treatment, which was okay with me.

I made sure the mortgage and utilities got paid and that there was money for groceries, clothes, and a few extras. Plus, I took care of the medical bills. Still, that wasn't enough. But even with the tension it caused at home, being a volunteer firefighter was one of the best decisions I ever made. It gave me a personal sense of

## A Memoir of Finding Love Again

satisfaction.

When the captain found out I could weld, he asked if I could build a device that would aid in extrication with more flexibility than the "jaws of life" alone.

"Can you make this?" he asked, pointing to a photo in *Fire Engineering* magazine.

I looked at it for a couple of seconds and said, "Yep. I can make it."

I wasn't as confident as I sounded. I knew I could make it, but I also wanted it to be perfect. That was probably my grandfather's influence.

Over the course of the next few days, I worked on a prototype from plans the captain gave me. I used the shop at the factory, mostly on my break time. It took a couple of nights to measure and cut the steel I'd bought. The next night I tack-welded it together. The following night I did the final weld. My boss stopped by to see what I was up to.

"Practicing your welding?" he asked.

"Yep."

"Oh, okay."

We didn't get to do much welding on the job, but we had to be able to weld anything at a moment's notice.

The nearly finished tool was a steel platform to be placed on a car's rocker panel, allowing hydraulic rams better access for disentangling car parts from a patient. I took the piece home to clean it up and added a coat of gray primer. The next morning, I stopped by the

# Trust the Timing

firehouse for coffee, got the piece out of the truck, and showed it to the captain.

"Here you go. This is yours," I said, handing it over.

"Beautiful!" I could tell he was pleased as he admired the workmanship. It went right on the rescue truck. Later, he suggested a couple of design changes. In time, I acquired scrap metal to build several more of the devices that went to various fire departments in the southern part of the county. I was not happy about being interviewed and photographed by the local paper about the device. I didn't want the attention. But I did feel good about making something that could help people.

My life was all about work, either paid or volunteer, with one exception: flying! I'd wanted to fly since I was about five years old when Mom took my brothers and me to an open house at the new airport. We got to tour inside a two-engine turbo prop that would hold fifty-eight passengers. Staring at all the dials and gauges, I figured the pilots must have been pretty smart to know what they all meant, to be able to fly an airplane.

At twenty-two, I'd pushed past my confidence issues and mustered up the courage to take an intro flight. I was hooked. Less than two years later, after forty hours of ground school and forty-two hours of in-flight training, I got my pilot's license, passing the flight test on the first try. I'd take that Cherokee Warrior and fly the daylights out of it, getting a natural high from training hard and acquiring proficiency and precision, proving to myself that *I was smart enough,* in spite of what my father said to the contrary.

Over the years, I worked as much as I could to satisfy my passion for flight. It filled a desire to go fast and master another skill. Flying provided an escape in a realm that was relaxing yet exhilarating at the same time. It was just me and the machine as one entity. Learning and enjoying the solitude of the sky, I felt at peace.

Things look so different at 2,500 feet. Things you think are big are not so big, like Block Island and Martha's Vineyard. And there's so much more to see, like the rocky coastline of southern New England from New Haven to Narragansett and the broad tapestry of yellows, reds, and greens in fall. At 1,000 feet, I'd see hundreds of seagulls feeding a mile offshore, the water churned up by bait fish trying to escape something deeper. The whole time I'd be listening to the aviation radio to make sure I was safe and feeling energized by my skills, especially when it came time to land, touching down like a feather. There truly was no time like flight time. I flew as much as I could until 1985 when I could no longer justify the expense or the time away from earning money.

My "rebellious" attitudes of expanding my realm were the beginning of the end of my eighteen-year marriage. I dared to want to learn new things. I didn't want to spend all my free time at home watching TV. I was in my thirties when I started to realize I had been living a lie. The more I tried to make things work, the less my life mattered.

## Trust the Timing

One night, after listening to a three-day litany about me not spending enough time at home, I'd had enough.

"Are you done?" I asked.

"Yep," she said. "I'm done."

"Good. I'm done too." I got up and walked out at 11:35 p.m., taking only the clothes on my back.

First, I went to the firehouse to get my thoughts together and decide what to do next. *Should I go back . . . and live the rest of my life feeling like a dog on a short leash?*

I decided to go talk to Mom. I told her what had happened and that I had left.

"I have my son back," she said. Mom knew how miserable I'd been for so many years, and she was happy for me.

Unfortunately, my mom didn't have room for me to stay at her place back then. I had to swallow my pride again and go to my father. I hated the feeling that I was begging him. But he just took me upstairs to one of the empty rooms and told me to stay as long as I wanted.

I stayed with my father for a year and a half to keep expenses low. He was glad I was there, but we still didn't see things the same. Our values were light-years apart. "You and your brothers should be more of a Christian like me," he'd say, watching his evangelical TV shows. Ten minutes later, he'd be speaking words of hate about some group of people. If that was what Christianity was, I didn't want any part of it.

It was fortunate that I worked every minute I could

because that meant we didn't see each other for long stretches of time. He didn't bother me too much until he caught me working on something or cooking, which inevitably resulted in him telling me, "You're not doing it right. Let me show you how to do it."

In 1995, after the failure of my first marriage, I gave serious thought to heading south. I wanted to get away for a week or so to catch my breath. It would be nice to travel to Jacksonville to see the changes. The thought crossed my mind again: *I wonder how JoAnne is. Is she okay? Is she happy?*

But it was a tough year. The state mandated that I yield 85 percent of my base take-home pay for temporary orders (alimony, child support, and contribution to household) for the next eighteen months. There would be no money or time for travel for a while. I knew I had a future, but the tomorrows were clouded in despair.

During this time of personal turmoil, I began to feel stirrings of my own spirituality. I didn't go to church because I'd heard too many scripture-quoting churchgoers criticizing other denominations, different races, and various ethnicities, but I knew I needed extra help to get through the day. Working maintenance on second shift, I took my break when I noticed the sun going down through the large window in the stairwell. I'd sit on a step and contemplate, trying to make sense of a life that kinda sucked and wondering how I could

## Trust the Timing

make it better. A silent prayer grew from this practice:
> *In the name of the Father and the Son and the Holy Spirit, I give thanks for the successes of this day and the opportunities. I ask for strength and wisdom to get through tomorrow, to make good decisions, to be able to hold my head up high.*

It worked. I felt a little better each day.

# 9

## *JoAnne*

# The Days Are Long, but the Years Are Short

### (1989–1999)

Not long after the miscarriage, we received a different kind of family addition. Brian's boss gave us a full-grown but emaciated German shepherd he found wandering the road. She was a serious dog, and I suspected she had never been socialized as part of a family. At first, she didn't wag her tail or put her ears back when we pet her, like most dogs do, but she would dart after a tennis ball and not give it back. Fortunately, she was not aggressive and just stared at our cat, Ramble, as if to say, *Run, cat, so I can chase you.* But aside from an occasional swat, Ramble ignored the new interloper to her queendom. I named the new dog Sarah, the name I had picked out for my second baby if that baby had been a girl. I'd been holding the name, not knowing what to do with it. And it seemed to be a good fit for our new family member who provided distraction from my grief.

## Trust the Timing

The baby was supposed to have been born in early June, and now I dreaded the date I had looked forward to. So when I read about the March for the Animals to be held in Washington, DC, on the same weekend as my due date, it was just the mission I needed. If I went to the march and made a project of it, I wouldn't have to think about the loss. I invited some other women to go with me and organized the trip.

Five of us drove to Washington and joined hundreds more to walk down Pennsylvania Avenue carrying signs protesting animal torture. My favorite sign was painted on a sheet held up by two young men standing along the side of the long reflecting pond. As I walked by, I read, "To harm any creature is to spit in God's face." It felt exhilarating to be with so many people who believed as I did, to chant with them that "Meat is Murder" and "Fur is Dead," and to listen to speeches on the Capitol lawn. For a while, I almost forgot that I was supposed to have had a baby that weekend.

My love for animals and the earth had always been strong. I felt more spiritual among the trees and in the ocean than anywhere else. Yet going to Good Shepherd Church almost every Sunday strengthened my appreciation for Jesus. I wondered how to incorporate my growing Christian beliefs with my strong spiritual feelings about nature. My church family accepted my questions with love. Someone suggested I read about Saint Francis of Assisi. That's where I found my connection.

## A Memoir of Finding Love Again

Saint Francis praised the sun and the moon, preached to the birds, and lovingly convinced a vicious wolf to stop terrorizing the village of Gubbio. I'm guessing Saint Francis didn't eat a lot of meat. Like the missing piece to a puzzle, the patron saint of animals relieved my theological tension and provided a comfortable way to connect my spiritual dots.

A quieter tension remained around the little hole in my heart. It had been three years since the miscarriage when thoughts about wanting another child rose to the surface. My analytical mind wondered if it had something to do with no longer using food to suppress my feelings. I'd lost sixty pounds in one year. People were concerned about my health, but I felt great. My goal, to eat only what I needed to be healthy, had worked. I'd eliminated all "empty calories" from my diet including candy, soda, and alcohol.

It was hard at first. Giving up all those comforts at once resulted in a month or two of mild mood swings, but I had a program and a support group to help me. Giving up sugar was just as hard as abstaining from alcohol. I've never considered myself an alcoholic but did my share of drinking, especially in college. With the responsibilities of my career and parenthood, I outgrew the party lifestyle, and my alcohol use had decreased steadily over the years. Working as a substance abuse counselor didn't technically prohibit me from drinking, but it was more comfortable to abstain. I wanted to set

## Trust the Timing

a good example and wouldn't want a client to see me out drinking and use that as an excuse. But the strongest motivator was that I wanted to lose weight.

Brian didn't join me in abstaining from alcohol. To his credit, he did not discourage me either and seemed to regard my goals with curiosity.

"So you're not going to drink *at all?*"

"That's right. No alcohol, no candy, no empty calories."

With abstinence from junk food and alcohol, and no longer eating whenever I felt like it, feelings I had suppressed rose to the surface. I longed for another baby.

My biggest concern about whether to have another child was my age. I was over thirty-five, the age when the risks of birth defects were said to increase significantly. I talked it over with Brian, who had financial concerns. Could we afford another child? But I knew lots of people had babies with less money than we had. I knew it wasn't logical. Yet the yearning to procreate isn't always logical. I kept mulling it over and did what I usually do when I'm unsure of something: I researched.

One evening at the library, studying the statistics of birth defects in relation to maternal age, I saw a boy with Down syndrome working on a computer with a woman who I guessed was his mother.

*That's not a good sign* was my first thought. But then I watched them more closely. They smiled as they talked quietly about what they were looking up on the computer.

I could see the love between them. My research told me that, even at thirty-seven, my chances of having a normal, healthy baby were still much greater than not. Seeing the boy and the woman having fun together at the library told me that it was worth taking the chance. I talked with Brian again about my desire, and when he consented, I allowed nature to take her course. I was pregnant within a month.

One of the blood tests they do during pregnancy was a bit off, so they did an ultrasound. For some unknown reason, the placenta had partially detached. They said it wasn't too serious but could result in an early delivery, so I needed to take it easy. I cut way back on my aerobics and prayed every day that my baby would be healthy. I ate healthy and indulged in daily banana smoothies and baked potatoes, being careful to cut out any bad spots in the potatoes that I'd read could cause birth defects.

Our baby girl was born only a few days before her "due date" in the middle of May 1993. When she came out, I asked, "Is she okay? Does she have Down's?" (I had decided not to risk amniocentesis.)

The doctor looked at me with surprise. "No, she has ups!" he joked. I breathed a sigh of relief.

We named her Ayla after the heroine in Jean M. Auel's Earth's Children Series, the prehistoric novels that started with *The Clan of the Cave Bear*. A couple of years earlier, I'd fallen in love with *The Plains of Passage*, the fourth book in the series, about Ayla's brave journey with her mate, two horses, and the wolf she thought of as a son. As I finished the book, I thought that if I ever had a baby girl, I might name her Ayla. I also liked the names Elizabeth and Alexandria, but Brian liked Ayla better. It rhymed with Layla, and he'd sing the Eric Clapton song to her, especially when she was fussy, replacing "Layla" with "Ayla."

I had enough vacation and sick time built up to be able to take off almost the whole summer with pay. It was wonderful to be a stay-at-home mom if only for three months. Big-brother Zack, at age seven, liked to help take care of his baby sister, for the first few years anyway. He was fascinated with magical things like breastfeeding and how the diaper service picked up the dirty diapers and delivered clean, fresh ones to our doorstep each week.

One hot and humid afternoon, Zack was outside playing with some neighborhood kids when it started to rain. I relaxed inside, nursing my baby girl and listening to the big kids sing silly songs in the rain. It was like a slice of heaven on earth. When Zack was born, and I was a new mom, someone told me, "The days are long, but the years are short." It was true. There was more work with two kids and time flew by, especially after I went back to my job outside the home, but staying home that summer with the kids was one of the best times of my life. I came to envy stay-at-home moms. It was hard to leave my little "Sweet Potato," as I called her, but we found a friend to watch Ayla for us.

## A Memoir of Finding Love Again

Both of our dogs were great with Ayla. When I was pregnant, I'd carried around a baby doll and told them sternly, "Be nice to the baby!" Then when I brought home the real baby, they knew that phrase and tone meant to be on their best behavior. Dobbs became even more zealous as a watchdog, bounding back and forth while barking in a deep voice at mail carriers, meter readers, and trash collectors. But Dobbs was terrified of thunder and fireworks.

One Fourth of July, when Ayla was about three, Dobbs must have panicked during the fireworks going off a few miles away and squeezed out of the gate. He didn't come back home until the next day. After that, we tried to keep him inside during fireworks and storms. But in August of 1999, when I was at work, he escaped from the backyard during a bad thunderstorm. When he didn't come home the next day, I started putting up flyers in our neighborhood and then in surrounding neighborhoods. I kept the front gate open. Brian checked at the pound every day. We cancelled our plans to go out of town for our anniversary. I couldn't leave with Dobbs missing. The longer he was gone, the more worried I became that he wouldn't come back.

After a few days, I went out in the backyard and knelt down with my hands on the earth. I prayed for Dobbs to be okay and for him to come home. I felt a sudden wave of sadness, fear, and dread, which made me think that Dobbs was dead. Brian came out to try to comfort me,

## Trust the Timing

and I eventually went back inside, having used up my tears, and tried to begin the process of accepting the loss.

The next morning was Saturday. Zack went out front and found Dobbs resting in the yard. He was okay except for a slight limp. I held Dobbs with tears of relief and gratitude. The kids danced around us with joy. Brian said it was like a scene from the old movie *Lassie Come Home*.

I wondered about those feelings of sadness and dread in response to my prayers. I had interpreted them to mean that Dobbs was dead. But was it possible that I had connected with Dobbs himself? Did that connection or my prayers help him get back home? Who knew? The important thing was that Dobbs was safe, and our family was back together.

## 10

*David*

# Just Work Harder!
(1995–2005)

Strict temporary orders for alimony and child support kept me close to home for the next year or so. I didn't mind paying child support. The rest would resolve later, but keeping my head above water required a lot of overtime and plowing snow. The winters of '95 and '96 were quite snowy in New England. I'd leave at the end of the snowfall and take about twelve hours to complete my plowing route. On each lot, I went back and forth moving snow to the right or left side, building hills and mountains of snow. I had to get creative figuring out where to put all the snow, especially when the snowfalls came back-to-back. The best time to plow was overnight in the peace and quiet with no traffic, even on the cleared roads. When sunrise came after an ice storm, the tree branches sparkled like jewels.

During one snowfall, I left the house at midnight and returned twenty-five hours later. That was a long day. Driving home at 1:00 a.m., I was so tired, I thought I saw

## Trust the Timing

vague shapes in the middle of the road that my mind said shouldn't be there. When I shook my head and refocused, the shapes went away. That night, I got three hours of sleep before going back out to finish plowing. Then I had to spread sand on the lots. My accounts included three fast-food restaurants, two doctors' offices, two banks, two churches, two firehouses, and one gas station along with a few private residences. I had to get the businesses done so they could open that morning.

Sometimes, I'd go straight from plowing to a shift at the factory. I could only do that for a couple of days, though. At the factory, I worked at least fifty hours a week in maintenance. The long hours meant less time at my father's house, as I stored away money toward a down payment on a house of my own.

That spring, things really started changing at work. We'd been told that contract laborers would displace the maintenance crew I worked with. Around the time the contractors were brought in "to help out," I saw a posting about an opening at the site fire department, and I jumped on it. I'd been working as a volunteer firefighter for eight years and had all the required certifications but one: EMT.

The chief was hesitant because I lacked the EMT certification. But I did well in my interview with the supervisor. One question asked was, "Why is a forty-year-old looking to be a career firefighter?"

I told them I wanted to make a difference.

## A Memoir of Finding Love Again

I was awarded the position contingent on my successful completion of the EMT course.

My confidence issue reared up, and I wondered if I were smart enough to pass the course. I studied hard, unlike in high school. I was a sponge. The class met two nights a week and some Saturdays from September through December. I was the next-to-oldest guy in the class. The oldest guy was sixty-two, a volunteer firefighter who ended up becoming a volunteer EMT.

A few weeks into the course, the three high school kids sitting behind me kept talking and joking during the lectures. After a while, I'd had enough. I raised my hand and said to the instructor, "Clint, hold on for a minute." Then I turned around to face the kids.

"Maybe *you* don't need this class, and it's just a joke to you, but I need this class to keep my job. You need to quiet down right now. Do I make myself clear?"

"Yes," they answered with big eyes. "I'm sorry."

"Thank you," said the young lady in front of me.

The instructor thanked me later.

Whenever I had a few extra minutes, I'd take out my EMT book. On my days off, I studied for hours. We had to do ten hours of ambulance ride time as part of the class, but not much happened during my training shift. I wanted to be ready, so I scheduled extra ride time on my days off. From October until January, I must have gone on close to one hundred training calls. I learned that no two calls were the same, and I gained valuable patient-assessment skills. In January of 1997, I passed my practical and written test and earned my EMT certificate. It felt great to overcome another obstacle. I'd honed my skills and felt confident working in the back of the ambulance.

For the rest of the year, I worked at the firehouse at the factory and also for a local ambulance company. Averaging about eighty hours a week allowed me to buy my own home by November.

The two-story Victorian house, built in 1893, was in a quiet neighborhood near a river. My intent was to rehab the house and flip it, then move to another and repeat the process. The house had a small basement barely big enough for a workshop (where I would someday make wine racks, toy boxes for grandkids, and a four-poster bed with a picket-fence headboard). But first, I had to work on the house. I stripped and reconditioned the staircase, built new storm windows, added an attic ladder and new ceiling fans, and painted the whole interior of the house. I spent all my spare time working on the house until a new interest moved home repairs to the back burner.

In the fall of 1997, I started dating a lady named Melissa who worked as a technician at the factory. We enjoyed each other's company. She liked to cook and travel, and she spoke kindly with a soft voice. Melissa worked quite a bit, and, being a workaholic myself, I saw this as her having ambition. She was so nice and so honest, I thought everything would be fine. We were married about a year after we started dating,

Things went well initially. During our first summer as a married couple, we traveled to Florida. Though it was my first time flying commercially, being an airplane nerd, I knew the route. We would pass over Norfolk; make a left at Kinston, North Carolina; and fly off the coast of South Carolina and Georgia into Orlando. When we made the left at Kinston, I immediately thought, *Just one more time to Jacksonville to see the town again. I wonder how JoAnne is.*

Not long after that trip, we had enough money for me to take up flying again. I flew pretty hard for a couple of years, breaking in new instructors and having to repeatedly demonstrate my skills as former instructors left to fly for airlines or freight companies. The repetition was worth it for the incredible high I got from flying and for the proficiency I gained while flying in adverse conditions. I got my instrument rating in September of 2000, allowing me to fly solo in all kinds of weather.

One of my best flights was on a night in early December when the weather was perfect. I chose the single-engine Piper Archer to log certification hours because, at 2,500 pounds, it was a little heavier and had more power than the Cherokee. As Melissa and I flew back from New Hampshire, the sky was crystal clear and the air as smooth as glass. At 4,000 feet looking down the centerline of the Worcester Airport, I could see Portsmouth, Boston, and Providence to my left and

## Trust the Timing

Hartford, New Haven, and New York City on my right. Straight ahead was Norwich-New London where we were headed.

It was such a beautiful night with amazing visibility. Snow on the ground to the north gave the streetlights a soft luster. From above, each streetlight appeared as an orange or white glowing circle. Melissa didn't seem interested in the view.

"Wow, look at those lights! Isn't that cool?" I asked.

"Yeah, so?" was all she said. She didn't sound mad. I guess it just wasn't a big deal to her.

I loved flying. But it was still a very expensive hobby that our finances would not support for long. I always wished I'd pursued it earlier and gotten my instructor's certificate back when I first started flying.

In December of 2001, we took a road trip to Central Florida to meet some of Melissa's relatives at Disney. Driving down through North Carolina, I saw the signs for Rocky Mount and remembered the route to Jacksonville. I thought about JoAnne with her easy smile. Every once in a while, I did a web search of Jacksonville High School and the alumni list and joined Classmates.com in hopes of connecting with some of the people of my past. But the people I was looking for weren't listed. I didn't recognize many names, maybe because I was only there for a year.

Melissa liked to sleep late when on vacation, so I walked along the boardwalk around the lake in the early morning to catch the sunrise when things were cool and there were no crowds. I had not particularly enjoyed previous Disney trips, but on this walk, I began to recognize Disney as a successful business model. You pay a lot of money to go into the park, but a lot of free things come with it. There's a great deal to learn at Disney through behind-the-scenes tours and from a customer-service perspective. The employees and cast members were always smiling and welcoming. I discovered interesting environmental work going on with composting and hydroponics, which got me thinking more about eco-friendly processes and the composting I'd done years ago. *Maybe someday I'll have a garden again,* I thought.

Not wanting to wait in lines, I often did my own thing while Melissa and her relatives went on rides. This not only made the vacation more enjoyable for me but also reinforced that I didn't have to get permission to explore my own interests. I still enjoyed spending time with family at lunch and at the end of the day.

In spite of the vacation, or maybe because of it, I started to realize that I was not happy with parts of my marriage. I appreciated Melissa's kind heart and gentle demeanor. But it turned out we had very different philosophies about some things, like money. When I tried to engage in problem-solving strategies, asking her thoughts on what we could do differently, she would clam up and go to the bedroom. I didn't know what I was doing wrong and felt frustrated by my inability to fix the problems growing between us.

My career, on the other hand, was going well. If it was burning, bleeding, or leaking, I was in the middle of it. Every shift offered positive new challenges and problems I *could* solve. It was the best job I could imagine next to getting paid to fly an airplane.

The contrast between my work and home life was like living two separate lives. Coming home after a twelve-hour shift, I felt deflated as I walked through the door. I spent most of my free time in the basement workshop or watching sports on TV and trying not to think about money (with little success). The marriage disintegrated to the point of us being roommates who barely talked. On the outside, things looked fine, but inside, I felt like I was drowning.

## 11

*JoAnne*

# Ms. Responsible
(1999–2000)

I read somewhere that raising a teenager is like trying to nail Jell-O to a tree. It's a lot of work and subject to unimagined challenges. As an adolescent, Zack emerged as the kind of person who would have been more comfortable in an earlier, earthier culture, where he might have become a respected shaman or explorer.

During the summer before Zack started his freshman year in high school, I'd taken vacation time to be home with the kids for a few days just to relax in between their scheduled day camps. After lunch, Zack asked if he could go to the woods near our house with a couple of his friends. Exploring the woods was one of my favorite things to do as a teenager, so that was fine with me.

The first call from the police came late in the afternoon when Brian was still at work. The caller said Zack was in some trouble at an industrial site near our neighborhood and that I should come there immediately. I grabbed Ayla, buckled her in the back seat, and drove to the site. A fire truck and police cars sat idle at the scene. Several official-looking men stood around conversing in small groups of two or three. I stood holding Ayla's hand and saw Zack sitting alone on a curb with his head in his hands. As I walked toward him, someone stopped me.

"I'm sorry, ma'am. You can't talk to him."

"He's my son. What happened?"

"He's going to be taken to the police station. They'll call you later."

"But I was told to come here! What happened?"

"Well, they're still investigating, but he'll probably be charged with arson."

"What?" I couldn't believe it. Zack, still sitting on the curb, looked up briefly and then buried his head in his arms.

"It's best if you just go home, and we'll call you."

Realizing this was not a good scene for Ayla to witness, I went home to wait.

I called Brian at work to let him know what had happened. He came home within a few minutes. I don't know how long we waited, but it felt like hours. It was dark out when the phone rang. I answered. The police officer on the other end said a parent needed to come down to the station. It wasn't clear as to whether Zack would be released. They wanted to talk to a parent in person.

I told Brian. He didn't say anything. He seemed overwhelmed, sitting in his chair, shaking his head in disbelief.

One of us had to stay home with Ayla, and one of us had to go to the police station.

"I'll handle it," I said, grabbing my purse. On the drive downtown, I figured it was just as well for me to be the one to pick him up. After all I'd learned on my job about kids getting bailed out of consequences too quickly, I didn't want Zack to get off too easy if he'd done something wrong. I wanted details about what happened.

At the police station, Zack looked relieved to see me. The officer checked my ID and told me Zack was charged with arson, and we'd be notified about a court date. He said I could take my son home, or he could go to the juvenile detention center. It was my decision.

*How could this be happening to my son? Arson?* Zack had talked about maybe wanting to be a cop. He'd been a Cub Scout! This was not part of the plan.

"Can I talk with him privately?" I asked.

The officer led us to a small office and left us alone.

"What happened?" I asked.

"It was a tiny fire, like this big." He cupped his hands the size of a softball.

"I thought you were going to the woods."

"We did. We were looking for a place to build a fire. Then I saw this building. It was like an airplane hangar, but it was completely empty. I made the fire in the building, so it wouldn't catch the woods on fire. It was on a dirt floor. I made sure it was safe."

"So did anything in the building catch on fire?"

## Trust the Timing

"No! Just the sticks and leaves I used to make the fire. The building was *empty*."

"Why did you have to build a fire anyway?"

"I wanted to teach Mike and Brandon how to make a fire." He said it like it was the most normal thing in the world.

"Do you realize what you did wrong?"

"I guess I picked the wrong place."

"Yes, on someone else's property! You know you're grounded."

"Yeah, I know. I'm sorry."

I took my son home.

With a lot of deep breaths and daily prayers, I did my best to stay rational and positive as we went through the juvenile court system. It was embarrassing for my son to have a probation officer, considering I'd worked with some of these people in my job.

My son's PO reassured me there were cops and others in law enforcement whose kids had been in their program. But I still felt embarrassed. I was a counselor. I wasn't supposed to have a kid on probation. Thankfully, Zack didn't get in any more legal trouble.

The fire incident and having a kid on probation made me want to work even harder to prove my competence. I felt like I was supposed to fix people, though intellectually, I knew that wasn't true. People are responsible for their own behavior, but on a gut level, I still felt it was a reflection on me if my son screwed up or my clients weren't doing well.

## A Memoir of Finding Love Again

It was hard for me to not take everything personally and to apply the Serenity Prayer, like a tourniquet to my ego, to accept the things I could not change. I struggled to turn things over to a power greater than myself. I can't imagine how anyone could work with addicts without a higher power. Maybe if you're really good at emotional detachment, but then you risk becoming a robot. It's a delicate balance. Caring too much can make you crazy. But you have to care; otherwise, you'd find something easier to do for a living.

Working as a substance abuse counselor had a huge impact on my life. Along with the spiritual growth, the job fed my already-overdeveloped sense of responsibility, which contradicted the spiritual lessons I was trying to learn. I had trouble letting go. I worried about my clients and my performance. There was always more to do on the job: more phone calls to reach out to clients who were missing appointments, more clients who needed to come in after work, and always more paperwork. There were weeks when I could have easily worked fifty hours, but I had a family at home who needed me too.

At home, there was plenty of additional work. As the primary breadwinner in the household, I took care of the mortgage, utilities, and medical bills while doing my best to be a good mother. I was not without help. Brian provided weekly groceries, gasoline and a few extras, but from the time I graduated from college, it was my responsibility to make sure the monthly bills got paid.

## Trust the Timing

Looking back, I wonder how I came to assume so much responsibility. I was a few years older than Brian and had lived on my own, which gave me more experience in paying my own bills. But it was deeper than that. Perhaps I didn't want to be dependent like my mother. More likely, I was *terrified* of being like my mother. The subconscious mandate required me to make sure my kids had stability, so they would never have to get rid of one of their pets or have to move to a different state in the middle of the school year.

It was the classic hero role rising to power. In job-related workshops, I'd learned all about the roles children of alcoholics take on in their families. At first, I thought, *Neither of my parents was an alcoholic. Why do I have so many COA traits* (never feeling like I was doing enough, friendships always revolving around projects and causes, feeling responsible for everything, etc.)? In adapting to my mother's depression, I had taken on the role of the high-achieving "family hero" but with the underlying introversion of the "lost child" escaping into fantasy, reading, and art. It was that creative lost child who had been drawn to Brian, the easygoing artist, in those carefree days of college. But the demands of my job and parenthood brought out the hero in full force. I accepted this role with a twisted sense of pride but had no idea of the long-term implications.

I always felt like I should be working harder to save the planet, but between my job and my responsibilities

## A Memoir of Finding Love Again

at home, there was only so much of me to go around. I felt stretched like a tight rubber band being pulled in different directions.

When faced with a challenge, I would grit my teeth and become Ms. Responsible, telling myself, *I can handle this.* Every now and then, I found myself sitting on the kitchen floor crying from exhaustion and compassion fatigue. But most of the time, Ms. Responsible was the automatic response, like when I went to pick up Zack from the police station and left Brian home with Ayla.

In later years, I wondered if I should have asked Brian to go to the police station. Could I have squelched my tendency to want to fix the problem? Could I have empowered Brian more? Could I have been more fun? I don't know. I do know it would have been hard to hold back in a crisis. And back then, it never would have occurred to me because Ms. Responsible was in control.

Ms. Responsible took care of lots of things like putting our old German shepherd, Sarah, "to sleep" during the summer of 2000. We didn't know how old Sarah was since she was an adult when Brian brought her home, but she was getting pretty gray around her muzzle. She developed major hip problems and had a lot of trouble walking. Sometimes, her back legs just fell out from under her. It was a hard decision to make, but Ms. Responsible took care of it.

Watching Dobbs get old was much harder.

When Dobbs was twelve, we found out he had

bladder cancer. Every time he urinated, it took him longer and longer to do his business so that he stopped lifting his leg and stood there straining, his body tense. We spent hundreds of dollars on surgery, which bought him some time. Yet I knew Dobbs wasn't going to live much longer, and I couldn't imagine being without a dog. One day, I followed an impulse and took the kids to visit the pound.

The golden retriever puppy in the back corner was the only one not barking. He was four months old, about the same age as most of the dogs there. We almost missed him since he was off by himself. His quiet demeanor made me wonder if he was depressed, but he perked up when the officer opened the gate and put a leash on him. As we walked him to the get-acquainted room, he pulled away from Ayla and made a beeline through the lobby to the front door. He turned and looked at us as if to say, *I'm ready to go with you. Get me out of here!* But he had to go to the vet first to get neutered. We decided to name him Jesse.

The second day he was home, Jesse was very sick. He slept a lot and refused to eat or drink. The vet noticed a small mark on his tongue that suggested he might have eaten something toxic. Jesse was given IV fluids and sent home with us. He wouldn't eat or drink for days and looked miserable. He didn't want to move and had to be coaxed to go outside. I was afraid Jesse was going to die and just couldn't let that happen, not on my watch.

## A Memoir of Finding Love Again

Consumed by maternal responsibility for our newly adopted family member, I spent most of my spare time sitting with him on the floor of the back porch. I stroked his soft, golden fur and laid my hands on him, praying as hard as I could, wondering what else I could do. I didn't want to leave him and would have brought him into bed with me if I thought Brian would have agreed. In the shower, I told God I would go to church more and do whatever he wanted me to do, "just please don't let our puppy die."

After about four days, Jesse started to get better. I felt so relieved, so thankful. Another vet later told me that swallowing a small battery had been known to cause those symptoms in puppies. I promised myself that I would never bring home another puppy unless I made sure the house was completely puppy proof.

It wasn't long after that, in November of 2000, that Brian said he had something to tell me. In a calm voice, he asked me to sit down on the couch with him.

He told me he was leaving.

## 12

## David

# NO MORE
## (2005–2009)

In 2005, I shifted into full workaholic status. Work was easier than thinking about my personal life or feeling feelings. I figured if I just pushed myself as hard as I could, things would get better. So I worked a lot of overtime at the firehouse, making sixty- to seventy-two hour workweeks common. The shifts lasted at least twelve hours, and we were always on call, never knowing when we'd get "banged out" for an emergency.

We were not allowed to sleep during a shift, but we sure did some cooking. That's how I developed a love for garlic. Garlic fests lightened things up. I hadn't had much exposure to garlic when I was young. My father didn't like it, so Mom never used it. My appreciation for the bulb began right before I started at the firehouse when I began growing it in my backyard garden.

A few of the guys at the firehouse liked garlic too. We made garlic bread, beef and garlic over linguine, and garlic-laden American chop suey for New Year's Eve.

We made garlic-dill red potatoes, and once we made a garlic rib roast. It was not unusual to use a whole bulb of garlic for a dish. Oh boy, did we stink! The whole firehouse smelled like garlic. We loved it. Those who didn't complained. This just made it more fun, especially when we had beans with garlic and onions.

One afternoon, the captain came to me.

"You're gonna love this," he said. "I have to counsel you."

"What now?" I often got "counseled," usually for my opinions about administrative decisions that didn't fit with how things worked in the trenches.

"You're using too much garlic," he said, trying not to laugh.

I looked at him for a few seconds, deciding whether to let this get to me. Then I responded with a few choice words, and we both had a good laugh.

We waited a couple of weeks before we made fish with garlic and made sure to leave some in the refrigerator. Complaints continued, but there was no more "counseling" on the issue of garlic.

If we got a call in the middle of a garlic fest, we had to go. No time to find a mint. Once we got an EMS call in the middle of a spaghetti and double-garlic-bread lunch. We'd just sat down to eat when we got the call. I grabbed two pieces of garlic bread that had as much garlic as the average loaf. Even I could smell me. The patients were nice about it: "Did you guys have a little garlic for lunch?"

## Trust the Timing

Having a sense of humor was crucial in emergency services, even if it was just "gallows humor" to relieve the tension in potentially life-or-death situations. In emergency services, we saw things no human should see. But I loved the work of helping people. No two calls were alike, every day was different, and the adrenaline wasn't bad either.

Still, my job was not a sure thing. At forty-nine, I was the second-oldest guy in the department. I didn't want to lose the benefits that would kick in in a few years and hoped I could make it another eleven years, to retire when I was sixty. But a dynamic shift in the business model at the corporate level created an atmosphere of uncertainty. Hearing talk about shutting down departments, I knew I needed a backup plan.

When the opportunity to become a certified EMS instructor came in the early part of 2006, I signed up. The class was tough, but the prospect of having another career to fall back on in the case of a layoff was the driver. Besides, I found that I liked teaching, and I got better at it each time I stood in front of the class. It was at that time I began working at the local ambulance company again. It provided me with extra money, and I could keep my skills up to provide optimum patient care.

With my confidence in the emergency services field and a growing awareness of taking care of others, I became aware of needing to take better care of myself. I'd gained some weight with all the cooking and garlic fests and noticed myself breathing hard with exertion. I'd started and stopped weight-training routines at home, becoming frustrated with myself. It helped when we finally got the approval to work out during the twelve-hour shifts at the firehouse. Cardio fitness just makes sense when you have to climb several flights of stairs carrying one hundred pounds of gear and be ready to go to work when you get to the top.

Physical health wasn't the only thing I needed to work on. Anger was an issue I'd been dealing with for as long as I could remember. I never hit anyone or caused bodily harm, but I felt the urge to on more than one occasion. I could go from zero to frustration to blind rage in minutes, seemingly without warning. But, looking back, there had always been a chain of events like working too many hours and coming home to drama.

One night, the dog ate the cranberry-apple pie I'd made and left on the counter. That's when I put my fist through the door, and it exploded into pieces. I didn't see the poor dog for the rest of the evening. I felt bad about scaring her. It was embarrassing to have to fix holes and pick up pieces of demolished wood projects. I didn't like feeling like a ticking time bomb.

I had to learn how to keep my anger from turning into rage. That meant I had to unlearn some lessons absorbed from repeated childhood exposure to my father's outbursts, which came without warning. When I talked with my long-lost relatives, I knew there had to be a genetic component, but I also knew I had to take responsibility for my part.

## Trust the Timing

Alcohol, of course, had been a contributor in the past. I'd stopped drinking hard liquor back in the eighties because I didn't like the meanness it brought out in me or the headaches that came along with it. Mixed drinks became tonic water with a twist. In time, I outgrew beer too, realizing it tended to give me headaches, not to mention bloating. It just wasn't worth it.

With a clearer head and a little more maturity, I got better at figuring out how to prevent the rage. I learned that it was important to stay hydrated, eat right, and take my blood pressure meds. As I took better care of myself, my physical condition improved, and so did my mood. I felt more confident. I got better at working off tension and learning to walk away before the anger grabbed hold of me. Giving anger time to diffuse allowed me to take a more constructive approach. But some things couldn't be fixed. Sometimes I just needed to get away from the source.

When I was fifty years old, I went to wish my father happy birthday and take him a T-shirt I'd gotten him at Daytona. I was coming off the night shift and joining family members for my father's birthday breakfast. On the way to the restaurant, I felt the same knot in the pit of my stomach that I felt every time I went to visit my father. It was the same knot I used to feel as a kid when I knew he was on his way home and the same knot that kept me in my room as much as possible when he was home.

There were about eleven of us at the table. I gave my father the shirt, which he promptly gave to one of the waitresses. For the next forty-five minutes, I did my best to ignore the disparaging comments and hateful words coming from my father. I felt the tension at the table grow thicker with each negative comment. My father's criticism was nothing new. I'd lived with it for many years. But something had changed in me. I realized I didn't have to sit there and listen to it anymore. Finally, I decided I'd had enough.

"I gotta go," I said abruptly and stood up.

"But we haven't . . ."

"It's time for me to go."

I walked out, got in my truck, and started to drive home. I had to get some sleep before my next shift.

As I drove home, all those memories of being called "stupid boy" rose to the surface as I gripped the steering wheel. I wasn't a boy any more, and I wasn't stupid.

"NO MORE!" I yelled as loud as I could. "I've tolerated this for fifty years. I am not doing it anymore. NO MORE!"

A feeling of relief washed over me. I slept well that afternoon.

There comes a time when we instinctively know that we have to detach in order to grow. My father's criticism taught me to limit the time I spent with him. I needed to be around positive people.

I found plenty of positive people by getting involved with civic and business organizations where people respected and supported each other. These were people who wanted to make a positive difference in the community and who were willing to try new things. They encouraged my desire for personal growth and leadership skills.

At home, Melissa voiced concerns about me being gone so much.

"You're never here. You're always working."

"I *have* to work to pay the bills!"

Caught in the classic workaholic way of thinking, I couldn't see any way out. I felt like I couldn't do anything right. I couldn't do enough. I was teaching, learning, and working as many hours as I could all for naught. Working seventy hours a week didn't make things better. Even if I worked twenty-four hours a day, seven days a week, it wouldn't be enough. I became depressed for the first time in my life.

One afternoon, Melissa and I sat in the living room. I was trying to make an effort by watching TV with her, but my tension grew with each commercial interruption. Melissa didn't seem to understand why I was so stressed, why I couldn't relax and enjoy life. But to me, sitting there felt like torture when there were so many more productive things I needed to be doing.

"I'd rather dangle from the end of a rope than live like this," I blurted out.

When there was no response, I retreated to the basement to find some project that didn't involve the use of power tools. I wasn't contemplating hanging myself or anything, but I felt like I was struggling just to keep my head above what I imagined as a cesspool of debt. How much longer could I live like this?

In addition to the challenges at home, the first hammer fell at the factory. The production operations would be ceasing at year's end. The possibility of getting laid off led to deepening despair.

I remember at one point praying to God and asking him, "What have I done so horribly wrong to deserve this?"

The possibility of pardon came toward the end of the year when a trusted friend shared a rumor that I would soon be living alone. "I just want to give you the heads-up," he told me. "Melissa's going to be moving out around the first of the year."

I was not surprised by the rumor or by the way the rumor mill worked in our small community. The news actually brought an element of relief. I had been grieving for the inevitable death of this marriage for years. It had lingered on far longer than I could have imagined. People asked me later why I had let it go on so long if I was so unhappy.

"I made a commitment," I told them. "It was the proper thing to do." That was true. But I had also hoped that this marriage would work out.

We didn't talk about it at all. I didn't bring up the rumor, partly because I didn't want to cause trouble for the friend who informed me and partly because I didn't

## Trust the Timing

want to jinx it. I let it play itself out and focused on work. When Melissa moved out, my stress level dropped tenfold in less than a week. But there was still no time to relax. The mortgage was due, and I had plenty of work ahead of me.

# 13

## JoAnne

# Grief Can Make You Blind

(2001–2006)

I didn't see it coming.

"Will you and Daddy ever get a divorce?" Ayla had asked me a couple of months earlier. Her question took me by surprise until I remembered her talking about her friend's parents splitting up.

"No, sweetie, you never have to worry about that," I assured her.

That's what I'd honestly believed. Her father and I had been married for twenty years. I thought we would grow old together and travel across the country in an RV like my parents did after the kids were grown. Had my seven-year-old daughter seen something I hadn't, or was she just curious because her friend's parents were splitting up?

*How would I tell her I was wrong?*

We were sitting in the church parking lot, getting

ready to go inside, and tears started rolling down my face.

"What's the matter?" Ayla asked.

"I want you to know everything's going to be okay," I said, trying to compose myself. "I'm just a little upset. Your dad and I have some things to work on. We're going to separate for a while."

She didn't say anything at first. "Why are you going to . . . separate?" she asked. "Are you getting a divorce?"

"I don't know yet. But it's going to be okay." I tried to reassure her.

"Then why are you crying?"

I took a breath and pulled myself together. "I'm just a little upset. But I'm okay."

Initially after Brian's announcement, I felt bewildered, like someone had pulled the rug out from under me. As the shock wore off, a heavy pain in my chest made me wonder if there might be something physically wrong with my heart. On my way to work one morning, my chest hurt so bad, I detoured to the urgent care place. They did some tests and told me my heart was working okay. It was probably just acid reflux and stress.

*God, why is this happening to me?* I kept wondering. I'd worked so hard to be good—a good mother, a good person . . . I thought I was a good wife. I knew Brian and I had things to work on, like every couple, and I was willing to do my part.

But it was too late.

In the evenings, I waited until I got in the shower

to cry as quietly as I could. When the kids went to their dad's every other Saturday, I sat on the hardwood floor in the hall, in the middle of the house so the neighbors wouldn't hear, and let the grief come out however it needed to. Getting started was the hardest part, like opening a tender wound that needed cleaning. When I didn't want to go there but knew I needed to cry, I'd start by humming. Sooner or later, the hum would become a moan.

As the pain emerged, I reminded myself to take slow, deep breaths in between sobs to keep my chest from hurting. The sobs sometimes turned to wailing as I rocked back and forth. Finally, I learned to let the sobs become a chant from deep in my throat, like the primal sounds of Native Americans singing with the steady beat of a drum as they danced around the fire. Afterward I felt drained but cleansed, still sad but not so knotted up.

I reminded myself that this grief process would take time. When I learned in my divorce support group that it takes one year of healing for every five years of marriage, I thought, *Great! I have to go through this for four years?* But the group offered hope too, like the Bible verse from Jeremiah 29:11 (NIV):

> "For I know the plans I have for you," declares the Lord, "plans to prosper you and not to harm you, plans to give you hope and a future."

I put that verse up on my refrigerator. I bought a coffee mug with the verse written on it and used that mug until it broke. Then I glued it back together and used it to hold pencils and pens.

The support group showed me that I was not alone and that I was not the only one watching way too much TV late into the night to distract myself, to avoid crawling into an empty bed to stare at the ceiling. I watched everything from science fiction to sitcom reruns like *The Golden Girls*. Could I live with a bunch of old ladies in my old age? They looked like they were having fun and supporting each other. *Maybe I could be okay with that*, I told myself.

When I ran out of distractions and the grief became unbearable, I ended up with my knees on the floor or in the middle of my bed with my arms wide open begging, "God, please, take this from me!"

Over the next several months, the pain got softer around the edges. I threw myself into painting, writing, and making collages from photos and magazines about the constants in my life: my family, nature, art, music, God, the dogs. I leaned into my church family, parents, and friends. Long walks with the dogs helped tremendously.

But that winter, Dobbs got worse. I kept him in the kitchen overnight because he couldn't control his bladder, and it was still too cold to leave him out all night. Every morning, I used two or three bath towels to mop up the kitchen floor. He was in pain, and I knew I would have to make a decision soon.

## A Memoir of Finding Love Again

I started to dig a grave for Dobbs in the backyard behind the grapevine where I had thrown my wedding ring a few days earlier. The grave had to be deep. With so many trees in my yard, I had to hack my way through thick roots. I didn't like hurting the trees' roots, but it had to be done. I had to be tough and not think about pain. Sweating took the place of crying as I vented my anger into digging, giving it to the earth. I thought about how Brian had complained about me "spending a lot of time with that dog" when I feared Jesse was dying. Well, maybe that time helped our puppy stay alive. Now, Dobbs was dying and I couldn't save him, but I felt a twisted sense of pride in proving I could at least dig his grave without anybody's help.

The grave digging took a couple of weeks. I did most of the work on weekends, or I'd put in thirty minutes after work until it was too dark to see. When the grave was at least four feet deep and about three feet wide, I scheduled the vet, who graciously agreed to come to the house.

It was a sunny Saturday in the middle of winter, not quite warm but not too cold. The kids went to their dad's, and I put Jesse in the house. Waiting for the vet, I brushed Dobbs in the backyard. His mostly black coat was soft and shiny in the sunlight. *Maybe I should wait and do this another day,* I thought. But the vet was on the way with his assistant, and they normally didn't make house calls.

## Trust the Timing

I watched while the vet gave Dobbs the first shot to literally put him to sleep. Dobbs went to the side of the house for a nap, and once he was well sedated, the vet gave him another shot. A few minutes later, when there was no pulse, the vet helped me put Dobbs on a blanket, and we carried him to the grave. The vet told me what a good job I'd done on the grave and was surprised I had done it all by myself. I held myself together well. I was good at that. On the outside, I appeared strong. Deep down, I was a wreck.

I did my best to stay busy, and there was plenty of work to do at home. For years, I'd done most of the yard work and house painting myself. But it was scary trying to reach the places at the very top where the roof came to a point, and cutting the thick hedges bordering the yard with a hacksaw and loppers made my hands ache. Even with Ayla and Zack helping, it was hard to find the time to keep up with everything.

In the spring, not long after the divorce became final, I noticed some landscaping being done at a house down the street, so I stopped to ask about getting my hedges trimmed. A tall guy with a good build, wearing overalls and no shirt, said he'd be happy to give me an estimate. The next afternoon, he stopped by and offered a reasonable fee for the yard work I wanted done. He said he'd get to it as soon as he finished with his current job.

After he trimmed my hedges, the landscaper, who

turned out to be more a handyman, offered to paint the most weathered side of my house. He also replaced a couple boards. A few days later, when the work was finished, he asked me out on a date.

My divorce was final. I had completed all thirteen sessions of the support group. I'd done plenty of grief work. I thought I was ready. Why not get out there and take a chance?

Grady was in his late thirties, several years younger than me, but he looked older—probably from spending so much time outside, or so I thought. On the surface, he appeared cool and confident, with his icy-blue eyes often accentuated by a five o'clock shadow. He was the type of man who might seem attractive at first to someone who is not well. I was impressed by his ability to fix things and his tan, muscular arms. I liked that he called me his angel and told me I could be a good influence on him. My drowsy intellect mumbled that I wasn't in any condition to be anybody's angel and that wasn't my job anyway. But I didn't listen.

There were many things that I overlooked about Grady. We were on the phone one night when the relationship was just starting, making plans for the next evening. Once we worked out the details, I confirmed with an enthusiastic "al-righty."

"Don't say al-righty," Grady reprimanded. "You sound like some kind of church lady."

I flinched emotionally. That must have been the

## Trust the Timing

moment when a chunk of my brain shut down, and my codependence rose up and grabbed me around the throat. I didn't know what to say. If I said anything, it was not even close to what I *should* have said, something like, *You know, I've changed my mind. Let's not go out at all, ever. Have a nice life.*

Unfortunately, that's not what I said.

It would be a long time before I said playful words like "al-righty" and "okey dokey," words that my new beau might find displeasing. I don't think it was a conscious decision but more a reflex to avoid rejection.

Even before that, I overlooked that he smoked cigarettes. *Someone can be a good person and smoke cigarettes,* I told myself. *I was a good person when I smoked cigarettes.* Nothing could get me to smoke again. I was confident of that. NO SMOKING EVER! was permanently carved into my brain. Maybe I wanted to prove it like someone might want to prove they could walk on hot coals.

I asked Ayla, who was eight at the time, what she thought of Grady.

"There's something wrong with him," she said, wrinkling her nose.

"Like what?"

"I don't know. There's just something *wrong* with him."

Ayla's instincts were on target. My instincts were completely overpowered by grief. My conscious mind was clueless.

## A Memoir of Finding Love Again

Laurel, one of my church friends, told me flat out she didn't like my new boyfriend at all. I tried to defend my choice. "But he *is* good looking, in a rugged kinda of way, don't you think?"

"Yeah. In a sick Marlboro Man kinda way." Laurel cut right through the crap, but I pushed her comment to a back corner of my mind where I didn't have to think about it.

Grady's tenacity when it came to sex didn't help. Maybe he had too much testosterone, or maybe sex was his way of controlling me. Either way, his persistence was hard to resist. Men like Grady might be good in a natural disaster or on a battlefield. But if I'd paid closer attention to my gut, I would have noticed that I didn't feel safe with him. The physically intense sexual high coupled with my grief and low self-esteem made the relationship downright addictive.

I didn't realize how vulnerable I was. Much of my grief came from having been unexpectedly discarded by someone who had promised to love me "till death do us part." On an emotional level, I felt unwanted and worthless as a woman, though I didn't believe that consciously. Maybe that's why I settled for the first man who asked me out. What should have been no more than a weekend fling ended up being a year of insanity. Not the fun, wild ride of insanity but the kind of insanity that still makes me cringe when I remember it.

There was no physical abuse. Grady was smart

## Trust the Timing

enough to know he couldn't get away with that. But the warning signs were there. I overlooked his ever-increasing jealousy and the tense feeling growing in my gut when I was around him. I overlooked that he drank more liquor than I first realized, especially when we were at his house. I even overlooked him putting his shaking hands around my throat without actually squeezing when he got frustrated.

To my credit, I did break up with him for a month but was lured back by empty promises about getting help ("I'll do anything you want") dressed up in brief, superficial change. How many times had I heard that story from other women in abusive relationships? I never dreamed I'd be walking in those shoes.

Trying to pull myself up out of the pit of grief, I'd grabbed hold of something sick and slimy and had fallen back down to an even deeper bottom. I discovered more codependent behavior than I would have ever thought possible for such a strong, intelligent woman as I had once been. My nerves were raw and constantly frazzled like a tiny mob of dancing puppets with a lot of broken strings.

One of the constants that helped me hang onto a thread of sanity was church. Grady went with me once or twice, but most of the time it was me alone or sometimes me and Ayla if she wasn't at her dad's for the weekend. I might have missed more Sundays while I was with Grady, but I never stopped going. My church family loved me no matter what. They always asked how I was doing and gave me lots of hugs. And there was the Good Shepherd himself.

One cold Sunday morning, when I'd been dating Grady for several months, I sat alone in one of the back pews on the verge of tears. Somewhere in the middle of the service, I became overwhelmed with grief and felt the familiar tight fist in my chest. I looked up at the Good Shepherd in the stained-glass window as he cradled the lamb in his arm. At that moment, love settled upon me, tangible love, as if someone had come behind me and gently wrapped a soft blanket around my shoulders. The feeling was so real that I glanced behind me. There was no one there that I could see, but, at least for that moment, I felt the security of being cherished.

Another thing that helped was water. In the summer, I swam in the ocean, usually with Ayla. When the weather was too cold or rainy, I swam at the YMCA. Swimming back and forth in a lane, allowing the cool water to caress my body, I watched the soft ripples moving out in front of my modified breaststroke. Sometimes, I'd swim or drift underwater, wearing goggles, to admire the wavy patterns of light playing on the blue bottom of the pool. Being in the water, whether ocean or pool, renewed my spirit.

One afternoon in parking lot, I ran into Tom, a former coworker who'd worked in construction before he became a counselor. He'd stopped by my house earlier to survey the work Grady had done and was not impressed. When I saw Tom at the Y, I mentioned to him that the relationship with Grady was stressful.

"You need to aim higher. You should be dating a doctor," he encouraged.

"Yeah, right," I said, rolling my eyes. I knew that being a doctor didn't make someone nicer than a handyman, but Tom meant well. He was trying to tell me I deserved better.

"You don't know how *cool* you are," he said, like it was something obvious.

Of course, Tom was happily married, but his words offered a seed of self-worth that landed in the remaining drop of common sense that had not completely dried up.

It wasn't long after that Brian, my ex, got married again. It was the final blow for him to get married so soon.

"Women grieve. Men replace," or so a lawyer friend told me.

Feeling down, I made the mistake of mentioning Brian's wedding date to Grady.

He peered at me like a hawk. "You *better* not be gettin' in bed with him," he warned.

"What? Why would I do that?"

"Don't play dumb with me. You want to get him in bed to try and change his mind." He nodded his head to confirm his accusation.

"I would never do that!" *How could he think that way*

## A Memoir of Finding Love Again

*about me? What kind of trash does he think I am?*

"Yeah, that's what they all say."

Grady's response baffled me. Obviously, that was not the place to seek comfort. So I spent the evening of Brian's wedding with my friend Deb. Smart, feisty Deb, who kept on loving me in spite of my temporary insanity.

Deb tried to talk some sense into me. "Grady should have told you he was going to take you out on a date tonight. He should have said, 'I'm going to show you such a good time you won't even think about what's his name.' He should have bought you flowers."

The seed of self-worth started to germinate.

My body rebelled against the stressful relationship with nervous fatigue, acid reflux, and mysterious female ailments. My gynecologist ran tests, which were all negative, and suggested various remedies. I confided to her about Grady.

"Maybe if you weren't under so much stress, your body would have an easier time healing whatever's wrong," she offered.

She was right. Trying to stay well when you're in a sick relationship is like constantly swimming upstream with weights. When it became clear that the relationship with Grady was making me sicker, I reached out for help and focused on my own recovery: going to meetings, reading, writing, and praying for some kind of relief, praying for mercy.

One evening, I took groceries over to Grady's house

for us to make dinner together. It was starting to dawn on me that, while he always had to know where I was and who I was with, he rarely came over to my house anymore. On our previous date, we'd had an argument about his jealousy. Maybe he sensed it was almost over.

Right after I put the groceries on the counter, he made an announcement: "I've decided I'm not ready for a relationship," he said.

I *should* have said, "Duh. You got that right!" or "You know, that's really interesting; *I've been thinking the same thing!*" Then too, I should have walked away many months earlier.

Instead, I choked back the tears. "You . . . don't . . . want me?"

I was still so broken.

Later, I came to understand that my response wasn't about Grady at all. It was about being rejected, *again*. But somewhere deep inside, I knew this "rejection" was a damn good thing.

I just walked out, leaving the groceries, even the asparagus.

As I drove away, the sky released a downpour.

Grady called me on my cell phone and asked me to come back.

"You're *crazy!*" I yelled into the phone as hard rain spattered my windshield. I threw the phone in the back seat.

A few minutes later, physical hunger gnawed at my

gut. I felt shaky. Not needing blood sugar issues on top of this, I pulled into a fast-food place. I was trying to be a good vegetarian, but I ordered a chicken sandwich and fries.

The storm raged outside as I sat down at a booth and started in on the fries. Looking around, I noticed I was the only customer in the whole place. I had to make myself slow down and focus on chewing and swallowing small bites of chicken sandwich that wanted to get stuck in my throat. As I sat there listening to the rain and eating my fast-food dinner alone, a soft wave of peace settled over me. It was as if my breathing had been restricted for a whole year, and now I could start to breathe normally again. The thunder and lightning outside would keep everyone else away. I was safe.

In time, I would realize that God had done for me what I could not do for myself. I remembered that shortly before his announcement, Grady had complimented me on losing weight since we'd started dating. "It's from stress," I told him. Maybe he realized he wasn't good for me. *I* knew he wasn't good for me. But why was it still hard to let go?

A woman in one of my recovery meetings suggested that I pray every day to let go of the relationship. So, I prayed every morning before I got out of bed. I prayed every time the phone rang, asking God to help me not return his calls. I reached out to the strong woman I had once been and let her drag me out of the pit. I listened

## Trust the Timing

to her when she told me I did NOT need a man badly enough to compromise my values or my health.

About a month after it ended for good, it was like waking up from a bad dream. Except it wasn't a dream, and I was in purgatory. The fallout of shame smoldered in me like a mild but lingering poison that took years to work its way out of my system. I gave myself plenty of crap for putting up with so much crap from a man who did not deserve me. *What was I thinking? How could I have allowed myself to put up with that for a whole year?* I didn't even have the excuse of financial dependence. I was an educated, independent woman, capable of providing basic needs for myself and my kids. Somebody must've hijacked my brain. Some spineless jellyfish, who I wanted *nothing to do with,* had trashed my psyche and left an embarrassing mess behind.

The truth is, I had forgotten who I was. I had forgotten my value. At the very least, the relationship with Grady taught me to have more compassion for people who stay in unhealthy relationships too long. Now I had to find compassion for myself. I bought myself flowers and encouraging cards. Along with swimming, I got back into yoga and meditation. I kept praying every day. And God sent me a present.

I had discovered a slow jazz station on the radio that soothed my exhausted nerves. But just as I was becoming a fan, the station changed its format to something experimental and not at all soothing.

## A Memoir of Finding Love Again

Stuck in traffic on my way home from work, I pushed the buttons on the radio, trying to find something relaxing or uplifting.

"I need a new radio station," I said out loud.

Then I looked up, and right in front of me I saw a bumper sticker for K-LOVE, a "positive and encouraging" station.

*Well I can't ignore that. Guess I have to give it a try,* I thought.

The lyrics were hopeful, the music light and relaxing. After a while, I realized I was listening to Christian radio. My experience with that genre was based on what my parents listened to—an old-time gospel/country sound that just wasn't my cup of tea. But this station was different. The music sounded like rock, pop, and R&B. And there were no commercials. So I gave K-LOVE a chance. Before long, I was singing new songs along with the radio, songs that reminded me I was loved by someone who would never leave me.

...

It was a time of transition for my little family. Zack wanted the freedom of adulthood with little inkling of how to carry out the responsibilities. A year earlier, he'd called me at work.

"Mom, I can't take it anymore."

"You can't take what?" I asked, though I had a pretty good idea.

## Trust the Timing

"I can't take school anymore. I can't take the people. It's too much."

He was doing okay academically, but after years of being picked on, he'd had enough.

"You know you have to go to school somewhere."

"I know. I'll go to night school or get my GED. I can't take high school anymore."

I cried in the school office the next day when I went to sign him out. I never thought one of my kids would drop out of school.

"It'll be okay, Mom," Zack assured me. He enrolled in the next semester of night school at the community college to get his high school diploma. It was the best decision he could have made. His grades were better, and he graduated earlier than his peers without all the angst.

After graduating from night school, Zack worked minimum-wage jobs. I let one of his friends stay in the tiny room off our living room for a while. *The more the merrier,* I thought. Having teenagers in the house distracted me from loneliness until their clutter pushed the limits of my two-bedroom house, and Zack's desire for grown-up freedom made it time for him to leave the nest.

Then it was just me and Ayla and our two dogs. During the rebound with Grady, I'd gotten Ayla a new puppy from the pound, a terrier/beagle mix we named Marigold. We called her Mary for short. While Mary was part of the quest for more merriment, I can now admit she was also an attempt to pacify my daughter, to make up for being so distracted.

As I approached menopause, Ayla ran straight into puberty. I'd known at thirty-seven, when I gave birth to her, that these would be challenging years. Now we were in the thick of it. Moods fluctuated unpredictably, and molehills erupted into mountains. Ayla started wearing lots of black and metal. I tried to get her interested in Christian heavy metal with only brief success.

She developed a dry sense of humor, reporting on bizarre things that happened at school like foulmouthed teenage drama queens fighting in the hallways; preachy teachers who were "too old to kill"; and how her science teacher, the one who made her take off her spiked dog collar, was demonstrating with a scalpel the location of an earthworm's brain and accidently flipped the tiny organ onto the desk of another student, which caused shrieking, panic, and ghastly rumors about worm brains. I didn't know whether to laugh or cringe.

"You could use stuff like that in a comedy routine," I'd tell her and gave examples of how to embellish her stories. She rarely thought my ideas were funny.

"Mom, that's not funny. But it's funny that you try," she'd say.

It was a game for me to try to make Ayla laugh or at least smile. Her smile would light up my heart, and we both won. Singing on road trips helped smooth out rough patches between us. Ayla taught me songs

## Trust the Timing

by Evanescence, and Pink, and later Lady Gaga (I love "Born This Way"). I taught her "old" seventies tunes, jazz standards, and Christmas songs. We both had a flair for Celtic songs and experimented with harmonies in "The Holly and the Ivy" and singing alternate lines of Simon and Garfunkel's "Scarborough Fair." Some of our best times were spent singing in the car.

When I missed having an adult partner, I wondered if there were any men with enough patience to even be on the fringes of this volcanic system of hormonal fluctuation. Out of curiosity, I went to a few singles events and practiced "speed dating," where you have about twenty minutes to ask each other questions before moving on to the next person. Speed dating was safe because I made it clear that I was only interested in friendship and made sure nobody followed me home.

One such event took place on a local singles cruise where women way outnumbered men and stood around in packs, surveying and whispering about the men. Sometimes they hooted as a lone man walked by. My reserved nature worked to my advantage, attracting a few prospects like the guy who wore a broad smile and a gold earring.

As soon as he said hello, I heard a voice inside my head say:

*He's not the one.*

The voice was clear and distinct, almost like my own thought but a tiny bit off to the side.

## A Memoir of Finding Love Again

The earring guy had a Northern accent, New York maybe. He told me he liked art, music, and animals before I revealed similar interests. We kept talking until the event moderator said our time was up.

"But I want to focus on her." He nodded to me.

"Well, I'll give you a few more minutes, but then you need to talk to someone else. This is *speed* dating."

We exchanged email addresses, which felt safer than giving him my phone number. Even if he wasn't *the one*, it might be nice to have a friend with similar interests.

When this new friend, whom I'll call Jerry, invited me to the art museum, I agreed on the condition that we'd take separate cars. After we toured the museum, Jerry walked me to my car. He kissed my hand and opened the door for me. Pretty smooth. For a couple of months, I told myself, *He's just a friend.* We went on friendly dates. I took Jesse to his house to meet his pit bull, Stella, and we drove the dogs to the park in my car. Another time, we took the dogs to the beach to let them run. The four of us became good friends.

Jerry was the most extroverted person I'd ever met. He talked and joked with strangers like they were lifelong friends. He was funny and lighthearted, great with little kids and dogs, and he made me smile. So I allowed myself to be courted, which led to us becoming more than friends.

Jerry introduced me to a church where the music team played the same kind of music I'd discovered on

## Trust the Timing

K-LOVE just a few months earlier. The simple music drew me in, and for a while, I had two churches. I still visited my Good Shepherd family, but on most Sundays, I went to the new church with Jerry. One brave Sunday, I asked about singing with their team. They invited me to rehearsal. Then they invited me to sing on the stage on Sunday mornings.

After four decades of singing only to myself, family, and a few close friends, I found the courage to sing in front of others. Jerry had brought me to a place that nurtured my musical talent, but he did not always support my budding confidence. I'd been singing on the stage for a few weeks when we were sitting at a table having refreshments after church. One of the church ladies told me I had a beautiful singing voice.

"Don't tell her that; she'll get a big head," Jerry interjected.

There was an awkward silence before someone changed the subject.

I wondered why Jerry would say such a thing. Was he joking? I should have asked him. But I just wondered.

Jerry was still a nice guy. He still made me laugh, though not as often as time went on. He had a good heart, and he fixed things around my house. With his amazing abundance of energy and extreme extroversion, he naturally talked a lot. While I could perform like an extrovert when necessary, I was still an introvert by nature, which made me a good listener.

## A Memoir of Finding Love Again

Much of my listening took place in what I jokingly referred to as my dining room, which was barely big enough for the three-foot-square table and four chairs. Sitting there after dinner, Jerry talked about politics, our educational system, and anything else he thought needed fixing. He talked and talked and talked. I listened and listened and listened. That got old after a while. It got to the point where I hated sitting at that table. I should have just gotten up to do the dishes or something, but I just sat there being a good listener.

About two years into the relationship, we were watching the Super Bowl in my living room. I have nothing against football, but it doesn't hold my attention for long. It was just the two of us, so I started doing a little yoga, making sure I didn't block his view of the TV.

"You don't do *yoga* during the *Super Bowl!*" He said it like I was crazy, like I'd just committed some awful sin. I went to the kitchen to finish my yoga pose, which I give myself credit for since it was better than hurrying right back to the couch next to him.

It took a few more months for my discomfort and self-esteem to build to the point of speaking up.

"You know, I'm really getting tired of your criticism."

"You just can't take it" was his response.

When he said things like that, I didn't know what to say. But I imagined all kinds of good comebacks afterwards, my favorite one being:

# Trust the Timing

*I could take it if I had to, but I don't have to. And I shouldn't have to.*

The thought kept running through my head, like a good friend telling me I deserved better and that I didn't need someone who added more stress to my life.

Jerry was not a bad guy. Ultimately, we were just two puzzle pieces that didn't quite fit. After dating him for three years, I realized that I still didn't feel relaxed with Jerry. I wanted somebody who could listen to me and support me as much as I did him. I wanted my opinions to be respected. I finally understood the saying "if it don't fit, don't force it" and broke off the relationship.

At least I was making progress.

## 14

*David*

# Know Who Your Friends Are

(2009)

In July of 2009, I was as broke as I had ever been with a big house, a bigger mortgage, and three dogs: "The Three Amigos."

Initially, I had not wanted any new dogs. Melissa and I had started out with two dogs and a cat. Then, two more cats came to live with us. The cats urinated everywhere, so I was relieved that Melissa took the cats with her when she moved out. Our sweet corgi had to be put to sleep at age ten with cancer in 2000. The other dog, Sparky, made it to fifteen when she had to be put down in 2004. The biggest reason I had not wanted any more dogs was that I didn't want to get attached and then feel that sadness again.

I still remembered how it broke my heart when I had to bury Winnie the Wonder Dog back in 1990 during my first marriage. Winnie had been my buddy for thirteen years. She was overweight because of all the snacks the kids tossed her. But she could move fast when she heard my keys jingle to signal a ride in the truck. When Winnie was thirteen, the tumor on her throat got so big she couldn't breathe well. She couldn't walk up the stairs without wheezing and coughing. She got sicker by the day. One morning, I knew it was time. I dug a hole in the backyard and carried her to the truck for what would be her last ride to the vet. She curled up in the middle of the seat and put her head in my lap like she had done so many times.

The vet said, "I think it's time."

"Me too," I said.

I wrapped her still body in her blanket and took her home. I laid her carefully in the three-foot-deep hole I'd dug in the earth and covered her with dirt as I sobbed my heart out.

After Winnie, I never wanted any more dogs. Melissa and I were both working twelve-hour shifts, an awfully long time for a dog to hold his or her legs together. We already had three cats and old Sparky. Adding another dog would make things even more complicated. But somehow, we ended up driving to Bridgeport to meet a puppy Melissa had seen online. The six-week-old little fluffball was the only survivor of a litter found in a dumpster. Her siblings had all succumbed to the parvovirus. She was timid and quite a cutie with mostly white fur peppered with black spots and a black face. On the way home, she curled up on the seat of the truck and went to sleep.

Beep, who was so named because her bark sounded like a car horn, turned out to be an Australian shepherd mix. We all suffered from her separation anxiety. If she wasn't kenneled when we were away, there was no telling the extent of damage she might do. Even when she was two and three years old, we'd come home to find remnants of shoes, clothes, canned goods, and other household items strewn about the house. I nicknamed her "Beep the Horrible."

One morning, I was taking a nap in the recliner after a shift transition, and Beep snuck quietly into my lap to snuggle. No dog, not even Winnie, had ever done that. Beep became my best dog friend. She was loaded with energy and always wanted to play ball. When she saw a bird or a squirrel, she took off flying across the yard like she'd been shot out of a cannon. It was her yard, and she knew it. You could see it in the way she pranced around with her head up or in the way she would lay with her front legs crossed in front of her like a classy lady. Beep was quite a girl.

Oreo, a spaniel mix, was a rescue out of North Carolina. He and his littermates along with their mother were to be terminated because their dad was not the intended genetic donor. Oreo began residence with us in July 2002. He and Beep became incredible friends from day one. He was this little wiggle dog who wanted

## Trust the Timing

everyone to love him. Oreo turned out to be a bit neurotic and part goat. He liked to eat nonfood items like socks, cardboard, foam rubber, and toilet paper whenever he got the chance. Undigested remnants were often discovered in the backyard. He trembled involuntarily when there were any loud noises, earning the title of "Oreo the Vibrating Dog." He was nervous around children but good with adults and not at all afraid of other dogs.

Then there was Dixie Doodle, a beautiful Treeing Walker Coonhound. She'd apparently been turned to the street early in her life to become a survivalist and was rescued from death row in Kentucky. Once again, I did not want another pet in the house, but promises were made to care for her, and the animal rescue organization brought Doodle to us in August of 2008. She was so thin, I could count every rib and the bones of her pelvis. She was reserved but somewhat gentle and friendly to people. When she got to the house, her survival instincts took over. It was like adopting an adolescent who has had to fight her whole life just to stay alive. She did not know how to back down from other dogs.

Oreo didn't like Doodle from the start. She was coming into his house, and she didn't belong. The dog wars ensued with early battles requiring repeated trips to the vet. Outside, the dogs usually got along fine, but if there was any competition for food, there would be a problem between Doodle and Oreo with Beep backing up her buddy.

## A Memoir of Finding Love Again

One injury came from Doodle trying to jump over the fence. She'd been able to clear the fence easily when she was thin, but after she put on weight, she didn't quite make it and needed stitches. The vet commented that I was coming in with a lot of injuries with this dog. With all the stress at work and at home, I was intolerant of his unfounded insinuations, so I went into alpha-dog mode and told him to formalize a complaint if he thought I was being abusive. He was decidedly nicer after that. Sometimes anger is useful.

Over time, the dog wars subsided. The dogs responded well to a structured routine with more consistency, especially at feeding time. Doodle got her food first in her room, the parlor with the French doors. Then Beep and Oreo ate in the kitchen. Breakfast was at four or six in the morning, depending on my shift. Dinner was generally at six in the evening. The dogs learned quickly. They showed their appreciation for the routine by barking to let me know when it was time to eat.

Doodle was our rooster, habitually waking up just before dawn and barking before the alarm clock went off. One morning, her barking sounded different to my half-awake brain. It sounded like she was outside. When I went downstairs, I discovered that Doodle had broken through a window. The loud part was hanging outside barking; her rear end was still in the house. At 4:00 a.m. she was barking to all the dogs in the neighborhood.

## Trust the Timing

Luckily, Doodle didn't get hurt that time, and I pulled her in before the neighbors complained. Though Doodle remained somewhat of a problem child, she mellowed with age and became an incredible friend.

The Three Amigos didn't ask for much. They were good companions at a time when I was in a rut emotionally. In marriage, I was zero for two. I was close to $10,000 in debt, not counting the mortgage. I spent a good deal of time looking inward, trying to figure things out.

I asked myself why I was such a perfectionist about certain things and so intolerant of mediocrity. Was it my upbringing, the constant tension provided by my father, or was I just wired that way? I became more tolerant of others when I recognized, *It's my life that I need to focus on.* I asked myself, *What do I do well? What do I need to improve in myself?* I felt Melissa had been off base with complaints that I was "cruel." But I needed to evaluate the feedback objectively. I could be focused and intense. I took pride in my work ethic. Was compassion a quality I needed to cultivate?

Those were the thoughts simmering in the back of my mind as I worked every minute I could to get back on track financially.

Going to the grocery store was a budgeting adventure requiring planning, strategy, and skill. I bought in bulk, cooked in batches, and ate a lot of pasta, rice, and peanut butter and jelly sandwiches. I experimented with marinades to treat freezer-burned meat. My typical grocery

## A Memoir of Finding Love Again

bill was twenty-five dollars a week including dog food. Needless to say, I didn't eat out much.

Mom knew I was working hard to get out of debt and would buy me breakfast a couple of times a week. We'd started spending more time together back in 2004 when she needed a walking partner to help her lose weight and strengthen her heart. We'd walk early in the morning, two or three times a week around Poquonnock Plains Park, and then we'd go to breakfast. At first, Mom and I took turns paying for breakfast, but as household finances became increasingly drained, there were times when I didn't even have five dollars in my pocket.

One morning I had to tell her I couldn't go out to breakfast because I couldn't afford to pay.

"You can't afford breakfast?" Mom asked.

"No, I can't afford it."

"I'll buy you breakfast," she said.

"Nope. I don't want you spending your hard-earned money buying me breakfast."

"But I like spending time with you, and you're helping me get in better shape."

I didn't want her to pay, but I couldn't afford to eat out, so I accepted gratefully and eventually was able to return the favor.

Sometimes, we'd have breakfast at Buford's Family Restaurant, a small café where I'd get the "Dishwasher Special" with eggs, onions, peppers, cheese, and Portuguese sausage. Other times we went to Puffins and had breakfast on the deck while watching the boats along the Thames River. Puffins was a nonprofit training restaurant for developmentally disadvantaged adults. Our favorite waitress, Emily, encouraged her clients with patience. She never raised her voice, no matter how many times she had to remind them how to take an order, pour coffee, or clear a table. I admired her compassion. Emily's kind and gentle spirit added to the comfort of the place. She shared bits of her life with us, and she and Mom stayed friends, even after Emily left waitressing to be a mother.

Breakfast with Mom served as my one purely social outlet. All my other relationships, with humans anyway, were work related. Mom and I laughed a lot, talked about current events, and exchanged updates on family, which included the dogs. She always asked about the dogs. Mom was good company.

The summer my second marriage ended, a trusted business friend called and said she had an idea she wanted to run by me. Jen and I volunteered together on a community project helping military families. Over the past two years, we'd developed a strong connection based on our like-minded, entrepreneurial spirits. We were the visionaries of the group and encouraged each other's ideas. So when Jen told me about the network marketing company she'd discovered, I listened. I felt her excitement and saw the opportunity for new ways of saving and earning money. My decision to join would open my mind to new possibilities and change my way of thinking, not just about business but about life in general. The company clarified a concept that I would soon become more familiar with: personal development. It came at a time when I needed it most.

During that same summer, I committed to the habit that has proven itself time and time again: giving thanks to God at the end of every day. At sunset, wherever I was, I gave thanks for my successes and for the lessons in missed opportunities. I prayed for the wisdom and strength to continue. Closing the day on a positive note set me up for more positive thoughts the next morning. Those two minutes of gratitude were incredible, bringing a sense of peace and hope.

The conscious daily contact drew me closer to God and strengthened our relationship.

"God, I don't know what you have in store for me," I told him, "but I'm ready."

# 15

## *JoAnne*
# Walk by Faith
(2006)

Jerry and I stayed friends after we broke up, and I kept going to the contemporary church, mostly for the music, until changes in the leadership made me look closer at a nagging discomfort. While the music and look of the place were contemporary and welcoming, the underlying theology was turning out to be more conservative than I had realized.

I found myself missing the inclusiveness of my Episcopal family. I missed the candles and the natural wood grain of the altar. Most of all, I missed the Good Shepherd cradling the lamb in the vineyard and the light shining through his red robe. So, after my three-year spiritual journey, I returned home to the fold and brought my guitar and some of the new music with me.

For the next five years, I didn't date anyone beyond the occasional coffee shop meeting or a platonic movie date. I'd finally learned to trust my gut when it said, *just a friend*. There were friends with conversation and friends on Facebook but no "friends with benefits" to complicate my life.

I tried to be cynical. I read books about the advantages of being single and all the things single women have accomplished. *Look at Mother Teresa,* I told myself. How would her life have been different if she had been married? Would she have accomplished so much good if she'd had a husband? *No way* was my first thought. But maybe if they had similar values and supported each other; maybe if they worked as a team—was that even possible?

Part of me wondered, *If I could find the right partner, someone who would be a good fit, someone I could relax and be myself with, would it be worth the risk?*

I went to a workshop on manifesting your dreams where we made booklets using magazine pictures and wrote in colored markers what we wanted to attract into our lives. The workshop leader told us to write our desires in the present tense, as if we already had them. I created pages about health, family, and career, and one page for my soulmate: he loves dogs and nature; he is considerate and loyal; he has integrity and a good sense of humor; and we respect each other's goals and are comfortable with each other.

I got to thinking about qualities I'd want in a partner. Maybe someone with family hero traits. I was tired of playing that role all by myself. Not that I wanted to be taken care of all the time, but it would be a relief to have a dependable partner, someone *capable* of supporting me emotionally and financially if I needed that. I'd married a mild-mannered artist who appealed to my own "lost child" but later brought out my overly responsible adult. The rebound with Grady had taken me to the other extreme of codependent madness. Jerry had played the mascot role with broad smiles and vivacious chatter. Hoping for someone "normal" didn't seem realistic. Finding someone *close* to normal, with some heroic leanings, might be a nice change.

At the end of the workshop, we were told not to keep bugging the Universe, God, or Powers That Be about our desires and that we would be amazed when things started manifesting very soon. But as the years went by, I couldn't help wondering what was taking so long. *What was my soulmate up to?*

This dry spell in my dating life gave Ayla and me lots of time together. For five years, our household consisted of just the two of us plus the two dogs. We weren't exactly best friends because I was in charge, most of the time. But our time together provided a foundation to carry us through the interesting years ahead when puberty and menopause would converge.

On the eve of Memorial Day in 2006, the air in our house was hot and heavy with hormonal irritability, so I took Ayla to the beach for a swim. We drove to Fort Fisher, a state-park recreation area, where no houses or condos would block the sun setting behind us. The water was so clear we could see our feet when we waded out up to our chests, and as we swam, the ocean washed away our tension.

All was well until we got back to the parking lot and realized Ayla didn't have her glasses. I pushed back the panic, thinking surely we'd find them if we just retraced our steps. We looked all over the parking lot, but it was getting dark. We searched through the Jeep, but the glasses weren't there.

"On your face or in the case!" I reminded her, feeling slightly sick in my stomach. "Those glasses cost $200 and have to be special-ordered. Next time we come to the beach, leave your glasses at home." She was supposed to wear them all the time, but it wasn't worth losing them like this.

My frustration was not only financial. Ayla needed her glasses more than ever in the week ahead for the almighty End-of-Grade Tests. Ayla, like her brother, struggled with school. Zack's decision to go to night school had turned out to be a good one. Now he was away at college in the mountains. Still, I hoped that at least one of my kids would graduate from high school the conventional way. Ayla couldn't afford to take the "EOGs" without her glasses.

I decided we would go back to the beach the next morning at the crack of dawn before anyone could step on them. That night, I said a prayer that we would find

## Trust the Timing

Ayla's glasses and they would be in one piece.

It was still dark when we got up on Memorial Day with that feeling of going on a special trip you have to get up early for. The sky lightened gradually during the thirty-minute drive to the beach.

We were the first ones there. We began our search in the parking lot and then retraced our steps to the spot we had laid our blanket the day before. All we saw was cool gray sand. We walked back to the parking lot and asked an early morning jogger if he had seen any glasses.

"There was a pair of glasses on a mile marker on the trail through those trees," he said, pointing behind him. "It's less than a mile from here."

"Thanks!" I got excited for a second but wondered what the odds were that the glasses had gotten that far. How could that happen overnight? It was a ridiculously long shot, but there were no other leads, and I was still determined not to give up. I'd been praying since dawn with that intense kind of praying that will give you a headache if you keep it up too long.

We walked from the beach through the savannah to the maritime forest and found the nature trail. The air was crisp and clean. It was still early and almost cool in the shade of the trees. We found the mile marker with somebody's glasses on top. But they were not Ayla's glasses. It was nice of someone to put them there though. I hoped the owner would find them.

Discouragement started to creep in as we continued

at a slower pace, and the trail looped back toward the parking lot.

"Look!" Ayla said, pointing ahead of us to the small deer bounding away down the trail. We'd been on this trail many times later in the day but had never seen any deer. It was a nice treat and lifted our spirits for a moment.

By the time we got back to the car, Ayla was dragging, thirsty, and ready to give up. I was NOT giving up until we found the glasses. I drove to a nearby convenience store and got drinks and hats because the sun was getting higher. We had not expected our search to take so long. I had expected that we would simply walk to the spot where we had put our blanket, and the glasses would be there.

"We are going to keep looking for your glasses until we find them," I told Ayla as we drove back to the beach. But when we got to the parking lot, she had had enough.

"Can I please wait in the car? It's so hot," she whined.

"*You* lost the glasses. You are going to help me find them!"

"We've already looked for two hours. We're not going to find them!"

She wouldn't budge. I thought about dragging her out, but a few people were arriving at the parking lot, and at thirteen, she was too big to drag without emergency adrenaline.

The morning sun was heating things up, and we had

## Trust the Timing

already walked for over an hour (not quite two), so I gave in and let her stay in the car with the windows down while I went for one last look.

I continued to pray as I walked from the parking lot to the beach, noticing what a gorgeous day it was. The water sparkled with sunlight, and the cool ocean breeze caressed my skin. It felt good to let go with my exhale, to allow a thin wave of acceptance to soften the edges of my fear. If Ayla's replacement glasses did not come in by testing day, she could go ahead and take the tests without her glasses. Then she could ask to retest when the new ones came in. After many years of advocating for my kids with the school system, I could make sure they let her do a retest. I took a few deep breaths. Then, instead of praying to find the glasses, I prayed, "God, just let it be okay."

I walked along the beach, enjoying the feel of the sand on my feet. Then I turned around to walk back toward the spot where we had put our blanket the night before. Just one last look. I saw only sand. I relaxed with another wave of acceptance, telling myself it would be okay. We would work it out.

Without thinking anything at all, I slowed down and slid my feet through the sand playfully, making semicircles as I walked. My foot bumped a small twig of sea-oat stalk, and I thought, *Wouldn't it be funny if I found the glasses this way, with my feet?* I slowed down even more and felt something else under the sand. It was another twig, and I smiled at myself, shaking my head. It would still be okay. I took a few more gliding steps and felt another little something with my toe. I looked down. Something out of place was sticking up out of the sand. I bent down and picked up Ayla's glasses. I stared at them in wonder. They were there all along, still in one piece, right under the surface near the spot where we had laid our blanket. They must have fallen off the blanket when we picked it up to leave. Overnight, a layer of sand had covered them. I couldn't *see* the glasses no matter how hard I looked. I had to relax, let go, and *feel* them.

Cradling the glasses, I sat on the sand and gazed at the vast ocean, letting its salty mist mingle with my tears of gratitude.

## 16

*David*

# Awakening
(2009–2010)

I had no idea what to expect. People kept telling me I just had to experience it.

"You know, if there's any way you can go to this conference, you need to go," my friend Jen told me. I wasn't sure if I could afford it, but it might do me good to get away. So I made plans to go to Florida in September of 2009 on Jen's recommendation. As the conference date approached, she warned me, "Be careful, Dave; this could make your head explode." Jen liked to use those kinds of expressions. She was full of energy and ideas with an internal drive allowing her to run multiple businesses while raising three kids and helping her husband with his business. She wasn't shy about telling you what she thought, so I knew her enthusiasm was genuine.

On the flight down, I felt excited to be headed to a place where I could learn, grow, and meet new people. As usual, the turn south over North Carolina brought back memories. I hoped JoAnne was doing okay. I

## A Memoir of Finding Love Again

remembered her smile and prayed that she was safe, happy, and strong.

The conference was like nothing I'd ever experienced. The atmosphere was amazing and the people incredibly gracious and nice. There were 6,000 people in the room and no poor attitudes. What intrigued me most was the company's emphasis on personal development with the encouragement to *be more than you think you can be*. People from all walks of life shared stories of overcoming obstacles. Their mantra was God, family, country, business—in that order—and no one was shy about sharing that. I noticed at the end of each presentation, the speaker closed with some form of "God bless you."

This talk of God at a business conference surprised me, but there was so much going on, I didn't think about it much at the time. Back home, the blessings I heard at the conference fed spiritual stirrings emerging from the past few years of questioning. At the same time, my practice of giving thanks at the end of the day began to include gratitude that I didn't have to be around negative people who caused me pain anymore. And then, my thoughts turned to forgiveness. I'd read somewhere that not forgiving wrongs done to me only harmed me more. I *needed* to forgive those who had done me wrong. I didn't want them to keep renting space in my head. I wanted to set that burden down.

I thought about my father. What had it been like for him going into World War II at seventeen, and his

## Trust the Timing

father dying six years before that? Did he have to bury his feelings and grow up fast? What made him sever his relationship with his mother? Why did he refuse to go to her funeral? And what did he see in Vietnam that gave him nightmares?

I remembered him telling me something about having nightmares a few years back. Since then, I'd learned more about PTSD and what it could be like to live with untreated. My father came from a time when soldiers just toughed it out, drank heavily, or both. He wouldn't allow himself to ask for help. This didn't excuse how he treated me and my mother, but it gave me more compassion and took the edge off my disdain for him. I'd taken comfort in the thought that my father would have a lot to answer for when he left this earth, but now, I didn't want any more harm to come to him. I wished him, and others who'd hurt me, all the health, happiness, and success they would be willing to find.

The peace that grew out of that forgiveness lightened my burden and allowed me to move forward. It was time to forge a new direction.

Every couple of months, I met my entrepreneurial friends at regional business meetings that started off with "The Pledge of Allegiance" followed by an invocation. Years previously, I would have thought, *You've gotta be kidding me; this is supposed to be business. Why do we have to have all this religious crap?* But it was different now. I was becoming more open to spirituality after beginning to explore it on my own terms. While I accepted my friends' commitments to their spiritual beliefs with curiosity, I wasn't ready to start praying in front of people. I had a personal spirituality that was just that: personal.

As the year came to an end, I was thankful to attain the goals I'd set in the first week of July. I'd promised myself to be debt-free by the stroke of midnight, December 31, 2009. And when the ball dropped, all my bills were paid with almost six months of reserve in the bank. Even the vet bills were paid up. The twenty-five-dollar weekly food budget, working all that overtime at the factory, and taking shifts and pager calls for the local ambulance company had paid off.

With my brain still in financial-repair mode, I maintained an attitude of all work and no play. The closest thing I had to a personal goal was to make a difference in the community. I continued to volunteer with the group that helped military spouses develop nontraditional businesses they could take with them when they moved. I served on steering and events committees of the local business association. At festivals, I helped people get where they needed to go and made sure the trash got picked up after the event. When someone asked for help with a task, I was glad to pitch in. If I wasn't working, I was there.

As a result of my volunteer work, the Greater Mystic Chamber of Commerce named me volunteer of the year. I felt honored to receive the award but uncomfortable

## Trust the Timing

going up to get my plaque in front of 150 people at the annual meeting. Thankfully, I didn't have to make a speech. Community service was (and still is) a natural part of my life. It helped me stay positive and sociable without spending money. It also gave me something like a social life. Otherwise, outside of family, my life was all business. I liked it that way.

My business friends encouraged me to read personal development books that made incredible sense. I felt inspired, excited, and affirmed in learning that my ideas about wanting to do and be something different were okay—that it was okay to think differently from the cookie-cutter complacency that some settled for.

Books like Napoleon Hill's *Think and Grow Rich* put into perspective ideas I'd had for many years about better ways of doing things, ideas that had been brushed off by supervisors with, "You don't need to worry about that; you're just a *factory worker.*" For years, I had been told what I couldn't do and why my innovative ideas wouldn't work. I was told I wasn't smart enough, I wasn't good enough, I didn't have a college degree. But those messages could no longer limit me. New messages were taking their place.

One conversation I had was with someone very dear to me. This person, with good intentions, cautioned me with all the reasons why my entrepreneurial plans wouldn't work.

I listened patiently for thirty minutes, then made a request.

"You've just spent thirty minutes telling me why it won't work; now spend thirty minutes telling me how it could work."

The silence was not a surprise. As a society, we are conditioned to worry more about what can go wrong than to imagine what can go right. A few months later, this same person commented on changes in my attitude, that I had become more positive.

I remembered a quote from one of the leadership books I'd read, "Our words have the power of life and death." Years later, I would hear the same message from the book of Proverbs, but before that, during this time of awakening, I was hungry for words of life. My whole attitude was shifting for the better. I'd still get knocked to my knees once in a while, but I could get up faster and with more determination. I learned to ask myself the hard questions about whether harsh comments and criticisms contained any truth or were only made for a cheap laugh at my expense. People could knock me down only if I let them. I could choose who to spend my personal time with. Family and coworkers commented that I seemed more focused, more confident.

Even my EMS teaching was starting to change. I liked teaching the stuff none of the other instructors wanted to touch like the respiratory, childbirth, and substance abuse modules. Respiratory was just a long module, childbirth was uncomfortable for some, and psych and substance abuse issues brought in all kinds of messy challenges. My beliefs about problematic patients were changing, and I found the confidence to share those beliefs. I reminded students that any one of these patients could be their mother or sister or brother. They were all human beings.

As I started to feel better about myself, I learned how to have more compassion for others. That compassion was about to be put to work.

In the spring of 2010, the Northeast experienced a once-in-a-century flood. I'd been pumping my basement for several hours when I received a call from my neighbor, Catherine, who lived across the street. She needed to go to a Rhode Island hospital for radiation therapy, and she had no ride due to the flooding. I was glad to be able to take her in my truck. She was safe, dry, and did not miss her appointment that day or the next several since I was on an eight-day break. Over the next four months, I made sure she could keep radiation appointments and provided what comfort I could by listening and keeping her company.

After the radiation therapy was done, I tried to check on her every day I had off. Sometimes we'd talk. One summer evening as she sat on her living room couch, she told me about her devotion to her church.

"I grew up in the church, but I don't go any more. Now I watch Reverend Robert Schuller on TV. Have you ever seen him?"

"No, I haven't," I admitted. "Tell me about him."

"Oh, he's very positive and uplifting. He gives me a great deal of comfort. Do you go to church, David?"

"I do not."

"You should."

I listened respectfully, knowing that this was important to her, though I was not interested in church. I talked with her about staying positive, because that's what she wanted, and helped explain what I could about her treatment.

In the third week of September, I was home cleaning when the call came in asking if I could take Catherine to the hospital. She needed emergency surgery to repair or remove tissue damaged during the radiation therapies. The timing was perfect since I didn't have to work until that night. I transported her to the emergency room at the Rhode Island hospital and waited with her for a few hours as they decided on treatment.

They closed the door of the ten-by-fourteen exam room to keep the smell of her dying tissue, burned from radiation, from permeating the emergency department. Everyone who came in winced at the smell and put on a mask. By that time, I'd gotten used to the smell and barely noticed it. When it was time for me to leave to go to work, Catherine asked if I'd pray for her. I'd never prayed out loud with another person before, so I was a bit unnerved by her request. But she was scared, and I wanted to comfort her, so I said a quick prayer for her and her doctors. She thanked me. On the drive back to

## Trust the Timing

Connecticut, I realized there were a lot harder things than having to pray out loud.

In the last weekend of September, it was off to Atlanta for another business conference. A month earlier, I'd gone to Dallas for a leadership conference and had been struck by a commonality all the speakers shared. It was their faith and its priority that stood out. I was beginning to realize this was a source of great strength for a lot of people. At the September conference, I paid more attention to the speakers and their words. Each of them, in their own way, gave thanks to God.

On Sunday morning, after the Atlanta convention, there was a nondenominational church service there at the hotel. Several of my friends in the company told me, "Dave, you really need to go to the church service." So, when I booked my flights, I scheduled time for the service.

At least two hundred people were there in the hotel conference room. I joined my friends from Connecticut in the front row. During the sermon, the pastor, Jess Gibson, who is vertically challenged and not a young man, wanted to emphasize a point, so he approached the empty chair to my left. As he raised one foot up to climb on the chair to stand on it, I put my hand up, giving him a pull point to hoist himself up. He then made his point—something about God's grace—got down, took five steps away, and stopped.

He turned around and said, "Did you see that?" Then he paused for a second. "Did you see that? Did you see what just happened? I didn't ask for help to stand on the chair, yet the help was there waiting. It was offered freely."

I felt I was in the right place. Staying for the church service had been a good decision.

When Pastor Jess asked anyone to come forward who was ready to commit or renew their faith in Jesus Christ, my brain told my butt to stay put, anchored to the chair. I wasn't going up there. I remembered how uncomfortable I felt when my father made us watch TV evangelists doing altar calls and flamboyant healings. But this was different. There were no TV cameras. Nobody was showing off. I watched a few people walk forward and stand in front of the pastor. Sitting in the front row, I didn't have far to walk. Just a few steps.

*It's time to do this.*

I stood up and walked forward. It felt odd, but it felt good too. I don't recall the exact words of faith Pastor Jess said over us, but I felt it was the right time to make a conscious decision, a commitment to go deeper, to open my heart and my mind. There was a feeling of peace. I was coming to my own spirituality in a way that wasn't forced or coerced. It was on my terms.

On my next Sunday off, I headed to church for the first time in many years. The little white church was almost 275 years old and perched atop a hill in the classic New

England setting. As I walked in, I saw many people from town I hadn't seen in years. It was a reunion of sorts. Everyone was welcoming and friendly. I'd met Pastor Dave earlier in the year at a business meeting. He was a kind man with white hair and bright-blue eyes. It was good to see him again. He had this way of making me feel comfortable with his gracious demeanor. The positive tone of his sermon reinforced my growing spirituality and the feeling of, again, being in the right place at the right time. I went to church for the remainder of the year as my schedule would allow. By the year's end, I was in a much better place mentally and spiritually.

Now when Catherine asked me if I went to church, I was glad to be able to tell her about going to the little church on the hill and how much I liked Pastor Dave and his positive messages.

"I know you went to church Sunday," she said to me on one visit.

"How do you know that?" I asked.

"I heard your truck leave at ten fifteen." She was quite smug.

I just smiled.

"You've been going to that church for a while now," she commented.

"Yes, I have," I replied.

"Would you ask your pastor to come visit me?" By this time, Catherine wasn't able to get up or walk without assistance. "I'm losing my strength. I'm supposed to be stronger than this."

"Of course, I'll ask him."

I talked to Pastor Dave about my friend and how hard it was to watch someone get weaker by the day. He said he would gladly go visit her.

"Guess who came to see me," she said a couple of days later.

"Who?"

"Pastor Dave. He was very nice and easy to talk to." Her smile told me how much the visit meant.

On the first Sunday in December, I came off the night shift at 6:00 a.m. and went home, hoping to sleep eight hours. But something woke me up early. I looked at the clock and saw I had time to get to church. With my usual holiday dread bearing down, I was not in a good mood and got up feeling empty. Over the years, I had come to despise the holidays. Growing up, the inevitable Christmas-morning arguments left me with memories of hiding out in my room until my father left and the coast was clear. As I aged, I became disillusioned by the commercialization and advertising blitzes that started the holiday season earlier and earlier. Material gifts of nothing heartfelt, along with the Christmas gift lists handed to me like a grocery list to take to the store, had taken away the true meaning of Christmas.

As I pulled into the church lot, I asked God for Pastor Dave to give me a message of hope. Then I put on my best face and headed into the sanctuary. Pastor Dave stood at the podium. I was impressed with how good he looked at seventy-nine with his kind blue eyes that shone with passion for his vocation.

"Let us now begin our worship with a message of *Hope!*" he began.

My attitude for the season changed right then.

Due to a shift schedule, accumulated overtime, and extending favors to coworkers, 2010 was the first Christmas I had off in eight years. I was blessed to be able to spend it with my son Alex and his family. My son Paul and his wife and kids came over too. The kids ran around in excitement while the adults got to reminisce about old times and catch up on news. I didn't have to watch what I said. There was no pretense, and no arguments broke out. Laughter and love filled the afternoon.

*I could get used to this!*

## 17

### *JoAnne*

# Finding "Me" Again: Midlife Adventures

#### (2006–2007)

The African drum circle designated the first Saturday of each month as "hippie day," which meant freestyle drumming and earthy songs. I made it a habit to be there. We met at Unity Church in a small group room or out under the trees, depending on the weather. Outside offered more room to dance. Theresa, the lovely belly dancer in her seventies, floated around the outside of the circle like a butterfly. She encouraged others to join her, and surrounded by so much acceptance, I let go of inhibitions and danced around the circle too, not as gracefully as Theresa but with a feeling of freedom. The group nurtured my self-worth, and I became comfortable enough to start a song when inspired by the drumbeat like The Beatles's "Let It Be" or one of the earthy chants I'd learned in a meditation class or from my beloved copy of *Earth Prayers from Around the World*.

## Trust the Timing

I tried an African dance class, which was exhilarating, though learning dance steps has always been a challenge for me. Improvisational movement with the downtown dance mobs was much easier and reminded me of the acting classes I took in college. The dance and drumming groups contained many of the same people. We met a few times a year for a potluck dinner and kirtan, singing Hindu chants about love and peace along with Native American chants and folk songs. It was a natural high, like going back to the seventies but without the drugs.

The drum circle, dance mobs, and kirtans were all part of my healing. I was exploring my own likes and dislikes with safe people, coming back to myself, and not just accepting but *embracing* my life as a single woman.

I returned to my environmental roots by volunteering to scoop up trash in neighborhood creeks and in Greenfield Lake—a good way to also get in some paddling without needing my own canoe. I attended local environmental meetings and joined grassroots efforts to fight pollution and save green space in our city.

I couldn't help thinking the environmental groups would be likely places to find a compatible partner since they offered a better ratio of men to women than dancing and drumming groups and certainly a better ratio than yoga classes. Not that I didn't love all those activities because I did. And not that I didn't like the company of women. At times, I much preferred the company of women—women who listened with acceptance and understanding, women who liked to dance and sing and laugh with loving hearts. Yet when I thought of myself with a life partner, I always imagined being with a man.

I chastised myself for evaluating the men I noticed at the environmental groups. I was supposed to be there for the cause, and I *was*, but it didn't hurt to keep my eyes open.

Instead of being so cynical, I started to treat myself to a few romantic comedies just for fun. I watched them not with yearning but with a positive lightheartedness that maybe someday the right person would come along. I paid money to go see *Must Love Dogs* at the theater because of the title. It was cute though dogs didn't play a huge role in the movie. I watched *Under the Tuscan Sun* on TV over and over again and loved the part about the town that built the railroad tracks long before the train ever came so they would be ready. Maybe my soulmate was busy getting himself ready for me. I imagined him sitting with me in the backyard and working in the garage/workshop that waited to be filled with tools, and sawhorses, and other guy things.

It was probably for the best that I didn't get into any romantic relationships during this time. Ayla and I still had our hormonally influenced skirmishes. As I entered the transition to menopause, Ayla slid down the back slope of puberty into her poetic Goth phase. Zack, flexing his independence hundreds of miles away in the mountains, had become distant emotionally as well as physically. I prayed for them constantly and for myself. I kept telling myself my daughter needed to be my priority along with working on me and getting my house in order.

It occurred to me that menopause was like adolescence but with more wisdom. Besides the mood swings, there were the "Who am I?" and "What do I want to do with the rest of my life?" questions.

The wear and tear of my job became more evident over the years. I worked hard to keep my sanity in an ever-growing maze of bureaucratic barriers, as the mental tug-of-war continued between my desire to be compassionate and the compulsion to be the "good girl" who gets A's on her papers. The steadily growing paperwork was like a pack of terriers constantly barking and nipping at my heels. I relished the time I actually got to do counseling or lead a group so I could focus on that one task while the paperwork terriers multiplied in my office.

Years of typing at the computer took a toll on my body. I started waking up every morning with my right thumb locked open, and I was unable to bend it without intense pain until it loosened up for the day. Cortisone injections helped for a month or two. Then I tried using the computer mouse with my left hand. It was slow going at first, but in time I got better at it, and my right thumb got better too. But a couple of months later, my left thumb started locking up. So much of my work was done on the computer, I was afraid I might not be able to continue my job. Finally, I asked for a laptop with a touchpad, so I didn't have to use a mouse. That was the answer. My hands and fingers still hurt at the end of a long day of typing, but I'd lovingly massage my hands with lotion, and the pain was manageable.

I had always known being a counselor would be challenging. I *expected* the emotional and mental challenges of working with people who suffered from addiction and mental illness. But I never imagined the huge piles of bureaucracy that would grow in my chosen field, or the resulting demands of so much typing, or the constant juggling and shifting from one skill set to another. *I'm thankful to have a job, and I can still do some good* were the mantras I used to keep going.

With the "Who am I?" questions of menopause, I remembered my love for the earth. I remembered that I used to be good at painting and drawing. I imagined someday spending my time doing work that felt more connected to helping people or the planet. I longed to work in a natural setting, where I could help people through meditation, art therapy, music therapy, or writing. My dream job would offer people opportunities for spiritual growth and connecting with nature. Or maybe I'd do something more basic like helping adults with reading and writing skills. Or, maybe someday, I'd be an *artist* again, if my hands would just hold up.

Books like *The Secret* about manifesting your desires gave me hope. Something about the steps of asking, believing, and receiving sounded biblical. Then I discovered they're

## Trust the Timing

right there in the twenty-first chapter of Matthew, verse twenty-two: "And all things you ask in prayer, believing, you will receive." (NASB)

My hopes and dreams came into focus at the Epiphany/collage-making party my Good Shepherd family had at the beginning of every year. We cut pictures and words from magazines about what we hoped for in the year ahead and glued them on poster board. I usually got so intense about my collage, searching for the perfect words and just the right pictures, I'd end up being the last one to finish while everyone else was dancing. But as the years went on, I learned to let go, with only a general intention of what I wanted, and used whatever pictures popped out at me. I always saved a little corner of my collage for my soulmate. "Must love dogs" remained nonnegotiable. Dogs had continued to be my most dependable and loyal companions. "Love me, love my dog," Mom used to say.

Jesse, my golden retriever, was my most constant male companion. I took him to Carolina Beach State Park at least once a year, usually in December for my birthday. We hiked through the turkey oaks to Sugarloaf, the giant sand dune. Being one of the few hills around, it was a bit of a challenge to climb straight up, until they fenced it off for preservation purposes; now you have to go around to get to the scenic overlook of the river. The redirection was okay since the more gradual slope came to be quite enough work as the years went by.

## A Memoir of Finding Love Again

While hiking along the trails, I loved to stop and look straight up through the tall pine trees on a clear day or watch how a slight breeze made the needles of the younger pines glisten in the sunlight. I loved to watch Jesse run along the marshy beach when (oops) the leash slipped out of my hand. I thought about how nice it would be to share this hike with a human partner someday. But I also liked the quiet independence of being just me and my dog. If I was feeling adventurous, we'd take a small, unmarked trail and get slightly "lost," enjoying the feeling of accomplishment upon finding a main trail again. Sometimes Ayla and Mary would come along, but usually it was just me and Jesse.

Ayla and I continued to share other adventures in a way we might have missed out on if there'd been a man in my life. She was becoming more rebellious, especially about Christianity, which baffled me at the time. I found an article online about goths for Jesus, which led me to the Revolution Church in Charlotte. It was time for a road trip!

We drove about four hours to a punk-rock club, where Jay Bakker, cofounder of Revolution Church and son of the once-famous Jim and Tammy Faye Bakker, the TV evangelist couple my parents had watched years earlier, was scheduled to speak. Jay had to cancel the visit, but we went anyway. We were welcomed to a potluck dinner by friendly young rebels with abundant piercings, tattoos, and multicolored hair. They shared the pain of

## Trust the Timing

being outcasts from mainstream Christianity. I bought a "RELIGION KILLS" bumper sticker from a young man who explained that people have killed themselves or been deeply wounded because of the way they had been rejected by traditional churches. "It's about a relationship with Jesus, not about religion," he said.

Graffiti covered the walls of the club, and a mannequin leg hung from the black ceiling. During the church service, people smoked cigarettes and listened to Scripture readings and Christian metal and punk. I think I was more impressed than Ayla, but at least she saw for herself that there are options beyond traditional church. The music was still playing when we left around 10:00 p.m., tired and ready to find our hotel. We ended up getting lost and drove around for about thirty minutes. This was before smartphones with GPS. Ayla was worried, but I felt confident and adventurous, knowing I could call the hotel for directions, which is what I finally did, and we arrived safely at our resting place.

Most of our other adventures were closer to home. Ayla joined me on a few local waterway cleanups. We fished plastic bottles, beer cans, and Styrofoam cups out of the lake as we maneuvered near foraging ducks and turtles sunning on logs. Once we found ourselves following a six-foot alligator who kept turning its head to look back at us while swimming away.

Our biggest paddling adventure was intended purely for fun. We signed up for a day trip with a group providing canoes to paddle to Zeke's Island. We started early in the day with clear skies and temperatures in the upper seventies. Once across the Fort Fisher Basin, we meandered around the marshy reserve. A soft breeze rustled the tall grass where we spotted white egrets. An osprey flew right over our heads. It was a perfect morning.

On the way back, the tide was so low, we had to carry our canoe a long way, with the mud sucking at each footstep as if we were wearing ten-pound boots. The others in our group got farther and farther ahead of us. After a while, we couldn't see anyone else. It was just me and Ayla and the birds and the mud. The sun reached its peak, and the temperature climbed toward ninety. The large aluminum canoe got heavier with each step.

We came to a narrow strip of beach and put the canoe down in the mud. I stretched my back while Ayla sat in the canoe. There were no signs of anyone else, no sounds but water lapping at the canoe and the soft wind. Squatting down to get a different perspective, all I could see was the green marsh grass waving in the breeze and the bluest blue sky with white clouds billowing above. I took my camera out of my pack to capture the beauty that gave no hint of our sweat and the sucking mud.

"Why can't we just leave the canoe here for someone else?" Ayla asked.

"Because it's our responsibility. We can do it."

"It doesn't even belong to us. They can come back

and get it."

"It's still *our responsibility*, Ayla. This experience will make us stronger," I said firmly, unsurprised by her eye roll. "And besides, we'd have to swim when the water gets deeper, and I don't want to get the camera wet."

"Why don't you just leave me here to die?"

Our eyes met, and we both laughed.

"I'm gonna throw mud on you," I threatened, and bent to scoop some up.

"Something jumped in the boat!" she shouted.

I looked and saw something small flapping around in the canoe.

"What the hell is that?" Ayla said.

"I'm not sure. It looks like a shrimp. And don't say, 'hell.'"

"Okay, that's a sign we should get shrimp for dinner."

Shrimp, being about the only meat I'd cook, was reserved for special occasions at our house, so it made an effective incentive. "Oh, okay," I said. "But no more complaining."

We got the creature out of the canoe and trudged on. The canoe wasn't quite as heavy with the enticement of a shrimp dinner.

I had a general idea of the direction, and after what felt like hours, but was probably more like fifteen minutes, we made it to water deep enough to paddle. We found the basin with signs of civilization on the distant shore. It took another fifteen minutes to paddle across as we watched the people on the dock gradually come into focus. We were both exhausted and glad to get back to the mainland. The rest of the group hadn't realized until we didn't show up that we were last in the line, so they were almost as relieved as we were.

On our way home, we bought two pounds of fresh shrimp, corn on the cob, and green beans. By the time we'd prepared everything, we were too tired to wash any more dishes than necessary and savored our shrimp dinner off biodegradable paper plates in triumphant silence.

Over the years, the memory of carrying the heavy canoe through the sucking mud in the midday summer heat and finding our way back on our own would become a rite of passage. Me and my girl did okay.

That night, I went out in my backyard to chat with God. I looked up at the brilliant full moon partially veiled by soft, gray clouds.

"God, thank you for being with me and Ayla today. I know you have a plan. I'm trying to trust you."

The symphony of cicadas, crickets, and frogs rose and reminded me I was not alone. The clouds parted, and the moon illuminated the grass where I stood and bathed my whole body. I moved so that my face was shadowed, so I could see the moon without being blinded, and breathed deeply of the warm night air. Then, stepping back into the light, I closed my eyes, arms lifted out beside me, palms open.

## Trust the Timing

"God, help me trust you."
*It's going to be okay,* said God.

>Journal entry: 8/25/07
>The moon tells me not to worry.
>Her light reflects the love of God.
>She knows I am a child of God,
>And a child of the Earth
>I am richly blessed.

## 18

### *David*

# Believe in Your Dreams
### (January–May 2011)

A field trip to Fort Lauderdale kicked off 2011. Once again, the turn over North Carolina piqued my interest. This time it was different: *I have a lot of vacation time to use. This summer, I'm going to Jacksonville.* I imagined going to the house where JoAnne lived in 1972 and knocking on the door. I'd introduce myself to her father and tell him about us dating in high school. Hopefully, he'd remember that I didn't cause any trouble. I'd tell him I just wanted to know if she was okay and ask if he would pass along the message that I hope she is well. I'd give him my contact information, just in case . . . I didn't imagine JoAnne lived in the same house, but there was a chance her parents did. I'd lost the address long ago, but I was sure I could find the house. It was all I could think of since I hadn't been able to find her online.

    I spent four days in Florida getting reacquainted with my older stepbrothers and their families. We had

## Trust the Timing

not known each other growing up. My father typically discouraged questions about them with a quick change of subject. It was great to compare notes and find out I wasn't as crazy as I thought. My stepbrothers had experienced some of the same challenges with our father that I had.

On my last full day in Florida, I headed to the Keys for a meeting with a business colleague. It was seventy-nine degrees on the sixth of January. Driving to Key Largo, the water was so clear I could see the white coral sand from the highway. And what a cultural shift! People had such laid-back attitudes. Nobody was antsy to get anywhere. I understood why people had gone there and never left.

I returned to a snowy New England on the seventh. It snowed quite a few times that January. Each time, I made my way to the church for snow removal. It was my way of giving back for the support I received from Pastor Dave and the congregation. I had the equipment, time, and experience, and it felt good. I'd try to do the plowing anonymously, but one of the church members who lived nearby caught me almost every time. Either Jim or Mr. Wingate would happen to drive by and offer to help me with shoveling the sidewalk and steps leading to the church.

I didn't mind plowing the church lot but felt relieved not to be plowing commercially since I'd started working at the firehouse. After fifty New England winters, I'd had about enough of snow and freezing temperatures that made my hands ache every winter. Beep was tired of snow, too. Each winter, it was harder for her to get up the three steps to the back door. On the coldest days, she didn't even want to go out. When she saw snow on the ground, she'd squint her eyes, put her ears back, and turn around to go back to the living room. I had to pick her up and carry her out to do her business, then carry her back in again.

Restlessness brewed inside me. I wasn't sure if I wanted to continue to live in Connecticut, New England, or move to who knows where. And what to do with the big old house I lived in? In late January, I went to a home show in Uncasville to get remodeling ideas. That's where I met Skip. He was a builder, volunteer firefighter, and all-around nice guy who always looked me square in the eye. He was at the show offering his home remodeling business and spoke with excitement about green building options.

Green building interested me, but something held me back. I felt uncertain about the future. "I just don't know if I want to invest that kind of money into this house or start over," I explained.

"Those are decisions you'll have to make," he said. "Take your time, and just let me know how I can help you." He didn't push.

"I'll keep you posted," I told him.

In our discussion that day and over the next few months, Skip became a friend I admired for his work in the community and his craftsmanship. I ran into him again at the Main Street Barber Shop in Old Lyme. As we spoke more, Skip shared about his journey. He told me about his struggles, personal choices, and relationship challenges. We had a lot in common.

"Things got better when I got more connected to my faith," he said. "I'm more at peace now. I've found things I was looking for. Things that were missing in my life."

I got the feeling from listening to Skip that I would do just fine whatever I decided to do about the house. I didn't have to stress about it. Things would work out; I just didn't know how.

By this time, the corporate business climate had eroded much of the passion I once felt for my full-time job. Bureaucracy and politics created increased levels of stress with layoffs all around me. I tried to ignore the tiresome dream-stealers in my head telling me, "you're just a factory worker."

One cold Thursday afternoon, I headed home to feed the dogs. I was supposed to be going to a motivational business meeting that night in Norwich, but I didn't really feel like going and thought about staying home. Going to the meeting would put me back home at 9:30 p.m., and I was already tired from a week of twelve-hour shifts. But I needed a pep talk. I knew I needed to be doing something different with my life.

Rounding the corner near my house, I saw the yellow-orange sun going down across the river and remembered

## A Memoir of Finding Love Again

to give thanks. I prayed for strength and wisdom. As I finished the prayer, the sun dipped below the horizon, and the words of motivational entrepreneur Johnna Parr came into my head:

> When your belief in you and your dream
> is greater than your belief in other people's
> opinions, you will have mastered your life.

That was exactly what I needed. *It's about my dreams and me this time!*

After feeding the dogs, I went to the meeting. My friends were happy to see me. Being with people who wanted to better themselves gave me the focus to move forward and define my own dreams instead of working for someone else's dreams.

I knew I wanted to fly again someday. Flying had always been a passion. Though I wasn't in a financial position to fly, just being around airplanes was like being a kid on Christmas morning. So when I saw that the second-largest aviation show in the U.S. would be held in March in Lakeland, Florida, I decided to use some of the vacation time I'd accumulated.

On opening day, I went hunting for "the highest-performing, safest, and most efficient single-engine piston aircraft": the Mooney. I found three, but no one was available to show them off. The weather had been horrible the day before, so fog had kept a lot of the displays from landing. I did get to sit in a brand-new Cessna 172, which was $300,000 worth of nice. It had the next generation

## Trust the Timing

of touch-screen avionics. But I still liked the Mooney. It was nice to dream. It would have been even nicer to share those dreams with someone else. Maybe someday.

From Florida, it was off to Kansas City for a conference where I learned more about developing myself and my leadership potential. I made new friends and learned valuable lessons from people who encouraged me as I rose from feeling like garbage to believing that I was just as capable of doing anything that anyone else could do—that with preparation, opportunity, action, commitment, and hard work, I could live a life of abundance. But it wasn't just about the dollar bill; it was about living a purposeful and deliberate life—not like a leaf drifting on the water but with a direction of hope and possibility. The conference brought me to a completely different state of mind. I had become *teachable*. Every nerve was aware with anticipation!

With this new energy, I started to notice things about myself. Emerging skills became clearer. When I was younger, I never wanted to risk being the center of attention because if I slipped up, there could be hell to pay. I just wanted to live my life quietly. But the uncertainty of my factory job had led me to push beyond my fears to become an EMT instructor. As I became comfortable talking in front of groups of people, students would come up to me after class or on the road and say, "Thanks for explaining it to me that way. It makes sense to me now."

I started to realize God had given me the ability to

teach in a way that others could understand. Reading John Maxwell's *Everyone Communicates, Few Connect*, I recognized how I could connect better with EMT students (and teach them to connect with patients as people) by taking into account different learning styles and presenting details that related to real-world experiences instead of just giving them the textbook approach. I taught not only how to apply an oxygen mask but also how not to let the elastic strap snap against the patient's cheek. I taught skills by the book, but textbooks don't tell you things like the conscious effort it might take to keep from saying, "eeewww" when you see certain injuries or that when you put a KED vest on a male patient, it only takes a couple of seconds to make sure the leg straps don't cause uncomfortable entrapment.

 I mentioned my new awareness to several people—instructors, students, and friends—and others mentioned it to me. They told me, "You know what you need to do? You need to be a speaker or a teacher. You know how to motivate people." The affirmation felt great! This was my calling, and I needed to pursue it.

 In the late spring, I assisted several EMT students in a study group. I told them I would not charge a fee but would work for food. We met several times, and they shared bits of personal information with the group. During one session, the subject of dating came up in reference to me. They were curious.

 "So, do you go out at all?" one of the students asked.

## Trust the Timing

"Nah, I'm not really interested. I'm working on *me* right now." Then, just to lighten things up, I added, "though it would be nice to keep company with someone for an evening . . . besides the four-legged companions I spend most of my time with."

"I have a cousin up in Maine who's got a friend who's divorced if you're interested," someone offered.

*Oh, dear God,* I thought. *They're trying to fix me up. Just what I need.*

"Alone sucks, but sometimes it's your best friend. It's easier that way," I explained.

"Dave, it's only a date!"

"No thanks. I'll be okay." I just wasn't there. I didn't need the liability of a relationship.

At the end of May, my finances were in good shape. I continued to work lots of overtime at the factory to get ahead. At the year's end, I'd be able to retire with full benefits. That was not my plan, but it was good to know I had the option. Working on my skills as a teacher and a business leader bolstered my confidence. The future was beginning to look bright, and I felt content with life for the most part, though every now and then, I felt like something was missing.

## 19

*JoAnne*

# Family, Friends, and Forgiving
### (2008–2010)

Mom usually answered the phone when I called my parents. But early in 2008, Dad answered.

"Your mom's taking a nap," he said. "She's been sleeping a lot lately. She hasn't been eating much."

Ayla and I drove to Jacksonville at least once a month to visit them, but I hadn't realized that Mom was doing so poorly. They didn't want me to worry, so I guess she made a special effort to be awake and alert when we visited.

As a kid, I wanted my mom to be stronger like my dad. Mom was kind, sweet, and romantic in the broad sense of the word. She collected angels and made "angeled eggs" for every holiday dinner. "We don't want to give the devil credit for something so good," she'd explain every time. I tried to avoid noticing that her mind was getting fuzzier as she got older.

## Trust the Timing

Mom was in her late seventies when she bragged about the red flower in a pot she kept in the living room. "It's been alive for months, and I never water it!" She beamed. She said it was a miracle and showed it to everyone who came to visit. I studied the flower and saw right away that it was plastic. I thought about it for a few minutes. I'd been reading about mental health being dependent on the acceptance of reality, and I'd been working to eliminate the remnants of my childhood habit of using fantasy to escape realities I didn't like. I figured I would want somebody to tell me the truth if I thought a plastic flower was real. So, thinking I'd do her a favor and set her straight, I said, "Mom, I think that flower is plastic."

"No, it isn't. It's real," she declared, as if I'd lost my senses.

"I don't know, Mom. It might be plastic. That would explain why it doesn't need water." I was trying to be logical, trying to make her mind work better.

She hesitated for a moment and then changed the subject.

As Mom got sicker, I was sorry I had told her the flower was plastic. I wished I had let her enjoy her little miracle flower. Why couldn't I have left it alone? Did I think it was more important for her to be correct than to be happy? Or had I just wanted Mom to be well? I think I wanted her to be strong because *I* wanted to be strong. *I* didn't want to be vulnerable.

Mom was in her eighties when she started having

trouble swallowing. Eventually, they put in a feeding tube because she lost a lot of weight in a few weeks. She was in and out of the nursing home depending on the severity of her condition. Dad took care of her when she was at home, cleaning her feeding tube and waiting on her. When she was in the nursing home, he visited at least once a day, often twice. I worried about them. It had only been a couple of years since Dad's quadruple bypass. Ayla and I visited them and helped as much as we could.

One morning in November, Dad called at about 4:00 a.m. He said that we needed to come. I drove with Ayla through the foggy darkness to the hospital in Jacksonville an hour away. When we got there, Mom was on life support. Her face was puffy, and her eyes were open but glazed over as if she were already far away.

"I love you, Mom," I whispered into her ear. "You're going to be a wonderful angel." Dad decided to go to the hospital chapel while they turned off the machines. I didn't know whether to stay with Mom or be with Dad. I knew this was the hardest thing he had ever done—harder than Vietnam, harder than losing Mary Kaye. I wanted to be with him.

As I followed Dad and Ayla to the hospital chapel, I remembered how Mom had gone with me to take Lobo to the vet when he had to be put to sleep. I couldn't even stay in the waiting room at the vet's and went to the car crying while Mom took Lobo in and stayed with him during the procedure. I thought of all the times over the years when she had sent me cards and little notes of encouragement or magazine clippings about whatever I was struggling with. Maybe Mom had been stronger than I knew, with a different kind of strength, even if it was a strength that depended on my dad being there. She and Dad had been quite a team, volunteering downtown at the soup kitchen, at their church, and with disabled veterans.

After Mom died, I worried how Dad would do. They had shared many adventures in their fifty-two years together, and he loved her so much. I wondered how he could go on, but he did. Once a Marine, always a Marine. After about a year, he got back to teaching Sunday school and living life, one day at a time.

As I got older, Dad became more open about his past. He shared colorful stories about his childhood, his adventures traveling across the country with Mom, and his experiences in the Marine Corps, though he had to stop talking about Vietnam because it gave him nightmares. When I was a teenager, Mom had hinted that Dad was having a hard time with those memories—a harder time than I wanted to know. It wasn't until after Mom died that I asked Dad what had helped him get through the torment of Vietnam.

"It was your Mother's love," he told me.

"What do you mean?" I asked.

"It was her compassion . . . her comfort. She would

## A Memoir of Finding Love Again

just hold me and stroke my head and tell me that it wasn't my fault . . . that the horrible things I had to do over there weren't my fault. She loved me through it."

The revelation floored me. As a teenager, I had thought of my mom as weak. Yes, she was nice and kind with lots of patience, but weak. Yet my mother's love was strong enough to save the strongest man I'd ever known.

My father's strength had always been a given. I'd heard stories about his tour of duty in Korea where a grenade had shattered his legs and hip. They put a plastic artery in one leg and left the wound open or reopened it so military doctors from Japan, Hawaii, Oakland, and the Great Lakes could look at the cutting-edge technique. He must have been some kind of patient celebrity flying from hospital to hospital as he followed instructions to squeeze saline into his open wound to keep it moist.

The plastic artery prevented him from getting a knee replacement as he got older. He was told the artery might not hold up, and there was a good chance he'd be paralyzed. The pain in his legs would have put most people in a wheelchair, but he kept putting one foot in front of the other, slow and steady with his cane. Every step was a challenge, but he kept going. I didn't want to believe that my enduring, gunny sergeant father might not live forever, but the reality that he was not Superman had started to dawn on me when he had his quadruple bypass, back before Mom got sick.

It was around the time of Dad's heart surgery that I'd

started talking more with Linda, who lived in California with her husband. I treasured our phone conversations, discovering a new abundance of support from my big sister's unconditional acceptance. We could talk about things we didn't want to tell other people. We found out that our parents would brag to each of us about how great the other set of grandkids was doing, but Linda and I confided in each other about how imperfect our kids were. And it was all okay. We talked about my love life, or lack thereof. Linda listened with love and encouragement. We talked about Ayla and I coming to visit her. Linda struggled with COPD and other health problems that turned out to be more serious than I realized. She died a year after Mom, in December of 2009, before we got around to making that visit. I thought we would have more time.

After Linda died, I imagined becoming the oldest person left in my family and still being single. The feeling of loneliness led me to appreciate the value of friendship with people close to my age and the comfort of being with people who knew me well. I wondered about my high school girlfriends.

I thought about Terry and our tenth-grade sleepovers, watching Johnny Carson and eating Cheetos, and how we rode our bikes all over Northwoods Park. And that party we had in her parents' garage where I met David forever ago. Terry and I still exchanged Christmas cards with short notes and pictures of our kids. In 2010, we started writing more about getting together. Through email, Terry helped me reconnect with Caroline and Sally. Caroline, who had invited David to the party in 1971, was happily married and living in Florida. Sally, the one who'd hung out with the coolest hippies and freaks, had worked for the government for several years and ended up with a successful career in banking. The four of us planned a girlfriends reunion at Wrightsville Beach, North Carolina, for September. We sent emails back and forth, preparing and planning our weekend with growing excitement.

It had been over thirty years since we'd seen each other. The reunion was filled with lots of laughter and plenty of catch up as we talked about the joys, sorrows, and challenges we'd all experienced. On the first night, we had dinner at the Oceanic, a waterfront restaurant, and walked on the beach. On the second night, Ayla joined us at the hotel where my girlfriends were staying. We cooled off in the pool and then went to the hotel room where we pulled out old yearbooks to reminisce about high school, old friends, and boyfriends. We filled in memory gaps for each other and shared the bits and pieces we'd heard about what ever happened to this person and that person.

"What ever happened to your first boyfriend, David?" Caroline asked.

"I don't know." Vague but sweet memories brought a

little smile to my lips. "I remember writing to him, but we lost contact not long after he moved."

"I remember you were pretty upset about him leaving," Terry said. "Have you ever looked for him online?"

"Yes, I have. But it's amazing how many people are out there with the same name." My thoughts of David were wispy scenes of passionate kissing and holding hands, talk of motorcycles, and Jethro Tull playing in the background.

Memories of another lifetime.

The girlfriends weekend wasn't nearly long enough. It felt like we were just getting started when it was time to say goodbye. We promised to stay in touch by phone and computer and to have another reunion soon.

That New Year's Eve, Ayla and I joined our friends Marci and Paul for a quiet evening of dinner, living room karaoke, and walking the labyrinth at the Church of the Servant. This labyrinth is a replica of the one in the Chartres Cathedral near Paris, built around 1200. The idea is that you follow the winding path of stepping stones in silent meditation, letting go of clutter and quieting the mind. When you get to the center, you might have a spiritual experience of illumination and then walk back along the same path, enlightened.

For once, I didn't have a plan for how the walk would go. I just knew I had to let go of resentments to make room for something better. I'd been working on forgiveness for ten years. For the first few of those years, all I could do was pray for the willingness to begin working on forgiveness. It was a long process of chipping away at a boulder full of anger. The boulder had provided security and distraction from pain, but now it was in the way.

The sanctuary glowed with soft overhead lights and candles. As I started the labyrinth, 2010 was almost over. The path twisted and turned in such a way that sometimes made me feel like I was going in the wrong direction. But it kept turning back again until, finally, I arrived at the center, where someone had put a box of tissues on the floor.

I closed my eyes and in a clear inner voice said, *I forgive you, _____*.

I said the name of each person I resented or felt betrayed by. I imagined each one of them standing there in front of me and told them I forgave them and wished for them to be happy. This time I meant it.

Then I included myself. I wrapped my arms around myself and said, *I forgive you. I love you.*

I felt God say, *You know I forgive you. I love you deeply. I want you to be happy.*

## 20

*David*

# You Never Know What You Might Find

(June 2011)

As summer approached, I was determined to take that trip to North Carolina, maybe in July. Scheduling would be a challenge because everybody wanted time off in the summer, but the new policy said I had to use all the time. There would be no payout like in years past. So I wasn't about to lose the time I'd earned.

My desire to travel and to live life more fully came partly from being tired of all the politics at work, but it also came from my neighbor, Catherine. She told me she'd always been careful with her money, but now she wasn't going to have the time to enjoy her savings.

As Catherine neared the end of her life, I visited her daily after work or in the evenings on my days off to make sure she was eating, and we talked to ease her anxiety. Back in January, she would call me and ask, "Are you going to come over tonight? I have a couple questions I want to ask you."

Over the course of a year, we had become friends. Catherine's tenacious spirit inspired me. She wouldn't let anyone say "cancer" around her. It was "the C word." After chemotherapy, she'd anonymously planted flowers and tended the garden at her church. She had especially liked to plant daffodils, hyacinths, and marigolds. She was frustrated when she became too sick to tend to the garden. Yet she still prayed and gave thanks for each day. After her radiation treatment, she was determined to only take over-the-counter meds, not wanting to get addicted, but she had no idea how much her tissue would deteriorate.

One spring evening, we were sitting in her living room. She was still ambulatory, sort of, and could sit in a chair. Her salt-and-pepper hair had grown back, but her body had continued to weaken. She was losing strength every day.

"I prayed to God for another miracle," she said. "I don't think he heard me this time."

"He heard you seven years ago in 2004," I said. "That's when you were given support and people to care for you so that you could have more time."

God had given her amazing strength from the very beginning of her journey. Her spirit, her will to stay positive until the end, gave me more strength than she knew.

I didn't know until later, when I got permission to get

## Trust the Timing

medical information, how fast the tumor was growing in her chest. In May, her hospice nurse told me how big it really was. The monster had spread throughout her thoracic cavity. I didn't know why it didn't displace parts of her body more. In spite of her positive attitude about life, Catherine's body was dying.

By June, she was on high doses of morphine and couldn't talk much. For me, it was about just being there, spending time with her. She had a live-in caretaker, but she needed a friend who didn't have to make her do things. It was hard to watch a once-vibrant human being fade away. It was just a matter of time.

After my hardest visits with Catherine, instead of going right home, I walked around the block to get my head on straight. I talked with God and thought about my own life and direction. I thought about what I wanted to do with the rest of my life.

*Where are we going with this?* I asked God.

I didn't get a clear answer, but I did get a sense of peace just by taking the time to ask the question, by putting it out there.

On my arrival back to the house, I followed the same routine: Let the dogs out; log on to the computer to check news, weather, and sports—maybe Facebook; and head upstairs to watch a ball game. This was my wind-down time to clear my mind and prepare for the upcoming day.

One Sunday evening, June 12, I performed my usual routine, but while on Facebook, I thought of JoAnne. I'd looked for her online many times over the years with no success.

*Let's see if she is on Facebook.*

I typed her name into the search bar, and nothing came up. Then I thought of Caroline, who had invited me to Terry's party where I met JoAnne in 1971. So I typed Caroline's name in. There were quite a few people with her same last name.

Let's take a minute and start at the top. Nope, not that one; second—nope, not that one either. On the next one, under hometown, was Jacksonville, North Carolina. The other info added up too. That was Caroline, all right.

Now then, let's take a look at her friends.

I glanced to the left of the screen and—"Holy S#*t!"

I sat back from the computer. Beep, lying on the floor next to my chair, raised her head and looked up at me.

"That's her!" I said, pointing at the computer screen.

"Thump! Thump! Thump!" went Beep's tail on the floor. *Dave's talking to me! He's excited!*

JoAnne was at the top of Caroline's friends list that night. I couldn't believe it. I pushed my chair away from the desk. "That's *her*, Beep!"

I had found JoAnne after thirty-nine years of not knowing anything about what had happened to her.

In the photo, she sat between two other women. One of them had to be Terry. JoAnne was wearing sunglasses, but I knew it was her. The long red hair that had gotten my attention long ago gleamed with gold in the sunlight.

## Trust the Timing

Memories emerged like snapshots—movie dates, holding hands, saying goodbye on the last day of school.

*So now what do I do?* I didn't know if she was married or what. I didn't want to intrude and complicate her life. I needed to wake up at four o'clock in the morning for the day shift, so I logged off and headed upstairs for the evening.

The next day, I couldn't get JoAnne out of my mind. Now that I knew she still existed, wonderful memories of the smart, beautiful young lady who loved me all those years ago flooded my mind. I remembered the softness of her red hair and the sparkle in her green eyes when she smiled her bright, easy smile. I remembered feeling comfortable and safe with her. I remembered how we respected each other.

Why didn't I message her? *Chicken!* Was I good enough to open a dialogue, to "chat" with her? What if I said the wrong thing? And then I remembered this question: "At the end of the day, do you want to say, 'I wish I had' or 'I'm glad I did'"?

I'd made a promise to myself at the start of my personal development journey to live a life of no regrets. Now it was time to live that promise.

That Monday evening, I logged on to Facebook with the intent of sending an instant message. I found JoAnne after a couple of minutes and sent the following message:

## A Memoir of Finding Love Again

Greetings to you!
After many years,
I hope you are well.
Take care and be safe!

Maybe she'll reply! It felt good and right to finally find her after all of these years.

## 21

### *JoAnne*

# The Power of Letting Go
#### (January–June 2011)

Someone once told me that everything she ever let go of had claw marks on it. I thought she was being funny. But over the years, I came to understand what she meant. I started to recognize my tendency to poke and pick at things after I'd supposedly let them go. Finally, when I knew I'd done my best and no amount of planning or worrying was going to help, especially at four in the morning, I'd turn it over, for a while.

When I felt lonely, I'd tell myself, *God has a plan.* I cultivated the belief that whatever that plan was, it would be good because I knew God wanted me to be happy. I knew that, as a single person, I could do good work and be happy. But I still felt a twinge of loneliness when I saw couples together at the beach or walking along the river at sunset, like I was missing out on something. I kept reminding myself that being single was way better than being with the wrong person. Sometimes I got mad at myself, thinking I was being weak and whiny. But my nurturing side (or maybe some angel) intervened: *Stop beating yourself up. You're human. It's a natural thing to want.*

I asked God to take away the desire for a partner or else send me a good one. "And God, I would really appreciate it if you could get my soulmate here before Dad and Jesse die," I added.

I knew I was strong enough now to deal with those losses. Even without a partner, I had proven to myself that I could cope with heartache and keep my head above water. No matter how much it hurt, I would deal with it, but I dreaded the thought of going through them without a solid partner at my side.

In the boredom of late winter, I caught myself looking again at a free online dating site and got annoyed. Some of the taglines men had on the free site gave me the creeps, like "Hot Rocket Man" and "Old Bull Full of Spice." And most of the men in my age bracket were looking for younger women.

*This isn't helping anything. It's a waste of time*, I said to myself, clicking the X and pushing away from the computer. So, once again, I turned over my desire for a partner, telling myself firmly, *Just focus on getting Ayla through high school.*

I made a promise to myself to stop searching, especially online, until after Ayla graduated. Then maybe I would go exploring and have adventures of my own.

In the meantime, Ayla and I had an adventure planned for spring break. She wanted to go to the national

## Trust the Timing

Holocaust museum, so we took a train to Washington, DC, and stayed with our friends Shawna and Rich, whom we'd met at a vegetarian potluck when they lived in Wilmington.

On our first night there, we went to the Washington Monument. It was a beautiful, clear night, and the monument stood out stark and eerily beautiful next to the full moon. The next day, our hosts drove us by the address on Oglethorpe Street where I lived when I was four. I didn't recognize the place without the front porch and hydrangea bushes. I hadn't even realized they were row houses, though I do remember the neighbors being pretty close. Things can sure look different after fifty years.

While in Washington, Ayla and I took our first subway ride alone. It felt daunting at first to us small-town girls, but we found our connection to our first destination: the United States Holocaust Memorial Museum. Walking through the recreated cramped "living" spaces, which were more like dying spaces, and studying the old black-and-white photographs helped us imagine the horrors of death and the courage of survival. We realized how much we took for granted. The Native American museum (National Museum of the American Indian) offered earthy sights and sounds, and the National Botanical Gardens delighted our senses with exotic flowers and lush foliage.

After arriving back at the subway station, we felt a sense of accomplishment as we waited for Rich to pick us up. An old man in a ragged military field jacket approached us. I figured he'd ask us for money, but instead he propositioned us for sexual favors. I told him we were not interested and to leave us alone, which he did.

"Well, I guess we've had enough adventure for one day," I observed.

"Yeah, that last part was creepy," Ayla said. She was starting to have second thoughts about moving to a big city. But it was a good trip overall, one we would always remember.

Back home, in the final semester of her senior year, Ayla had to pass a computer class to graduate. She didn't like the teacher and complained about her unreasonable demands. Later, she admitted she'd been slack for the first nine weeks. Recognizing what was at stake, Ayla buckled down and worked hard in the last two months, making hundreds of note cards and keeping up with her assignments. We worried about the state exam she had to pass for the class. I prayed about it, but I also planned how I could go to the principal with all the reasons he should override the teacher's grade if Ayla didn't pass: *Aside from the teacher being unreasonable . . . after all we've been through . . . with her ADD issues . . . and being bullied because she's different . . . and how she worked so hard and finally passed algebra on the third try. You can't let this one class stop her from graduating . . . Surely there must be some alternative.*

# Trust the Timing

I would take it up the chain as far as I needed to. I could do that.

As I explored options about how to intervene, some helpful person, a school counselor or social worker, revealed that the "unreasonable" teacher was battling a serious illness. That put a different light on things and softened me out of crusade mode.

A couple of weeks before the exam, it came to me to pray every day, not only for Ayla to pass but also for the teacher. It wasn't easy to just pray for the teacher without it being about Ayla passing, but I made myself do it with as much sincerity as I could muster. As Ayla studied her note cards, I envisioned the teacher surrounded by love and peace. I wished her blessings of healing. I sent her love. I prayed for peace between Ayla and her teacher. Then I worked on turning it over and having faith.

The day after the exam, restless to know the outcome, I sent the teacher a respectful email thanking her and letting her know how hard Ayla had worked and how I'd been praying. The teacher wrote back that she did not know her final grade yet but that Ayla's hard work and the prayer had paid off. Ayla made a ninety-three on the state exam. She ended up getting a B in the class and graduated from high school.

On the Tuesday evening after Ayla's graduation ceremony, I sat down at the computer with no thoughts or expectations except to check my email and to see what

## A Memoir of Finding Love Again

friends were up to on Facebook. There was a private message.

I clicked on the icon and looked at the name that took my breath away. I felt my heart pick up speed as I read the message. Then I sat back and took a deep breath. It had been a long day. Maybe I was seeing things.

Like a skeptical jeweler studying a diamond to see if it's real, I moved closer and read the name again. I had typed that name into the computer a couple of times but gave up after seeing how many people there were with the name of my first love. And besides, I was the one who wrote to him last in 1972, so it was his turn. Now, in 2011, he was finally getting back to me with this simple, friendly message that made my heart feel like it was going to leap out of my chest.

But was it really him? I couldn't find any pictures of him on his profile, just a photo of what appeared to be a small airport runway. But it did say he graduated in 1974, and there was Jethro Tull listed under his "likes." Of course it was him!

I could hardly contain my excitement as I typed:
> Wow! I knew it was really you when I saw Jethro Tull in your favorite music. What sweet memories. I am well, for 55 anyway. My profile picture is from the reunion we had in Sept with Sally, Terry, and Caroline, after many years of no contact. It's so nice to get your message. Hope you are well and safe too!

# Trust the Timing

I hit send, read what I'd sent, and rolled my eyes.

*Good grief! Calm down and get a grip. He's just saying hello. That's all.*

David was a good guy when we dated in high school, but so much time had gone by. He could have changed into . . . who knows what? And why wasn't his relationship status posted? Was he being secretive, or did he just not care to give out that much information? I decided to take a chance and send him a friend request. He was still far away. If he turned out to be a jerk, I could simply unfriend him.

As we progressed from Facebook to phone calls, he didn't sound like a jerk. He sounded very interesting. He lived in Connecticut and worked as a firefighter/EMT. And he had *three dogs*. When David talked about his dogs, I could tell he thought of them as family. I talked to the dogs on the phone and listened to them sing in three-part harmony with a rough bark, a long howl, and a yip, yip, yip. Beep was the barker. She was ten years old, almost as old as Jesse, and couldn't climb the stairs anymore.

"Yep, I carry the old girl upstairs to the bedroom every night," David told me.

My heart wanted to melt, and my toes tingled at the image of him carrying his old dog upstairs to bed. I constantly had to remind myself to keep my feet on the ground, to keep my ears open and my brain fully engaged.

As David and I talked, a tiny ember of hope, like a

seed that had been dormant and almost forgotten after so many years, started to grow. I asked a lot of questions, and he didn't mind answering them. "Nothing's off the table," he told me.

"That's good," I said, "because I have a lot of questions."

One night David had a question of his own. He asked me what I was doing on July 15.

"Well, I was going to visit my son in the mountains that weekend, but he's busy, so we moved that trip to August. Why do you ask?"

"I have some time off that weekend. How would you feel about me taking you out to dinner that Friday night?"

I was hesitant. Was he going to come to North Carolina to take me to dinner? *What if he just knows the right things to say? What if he turns out to be crazy?*

Then I remembered what my dad told me all those years ago, when I was twelve years old and didn't want to leave North Carolina: *nothing is impossible.*

*What if . . . ?*

"Are you still there?" he asked.

"You're going to come all the way down here to Wilmington, North Carolina, just to have dinner with me?"

"Yep, with one catch."

*Okay, here it comes. Be careful.* "What's the catch?" I tried to sound businesslike.

The catch wasn't a catch at all. He said he wanted to encumber my Saturday, to sit and talk, to find out what

## Trust the Timing

had brought me to this point in my life and something about sitting in the backyard sipping on lemonade.

I had to take the chance. I said yes.

It was a date!

## 22

*David*

# Reunion
(July 2011)

It was Tuesday evening when I logged on to the computer again to see if there was a reply. Reply she did! A nice message back and a friend request! WOW! This was neat! Of course, I accepted the request and was able to learn more about her. Her profile was interesting and made me want to know more. Maybe someday we could talk and catch up.

We went back and forth with the messaging function on Facebook for a while. Then I asked for her phone number. She sent it back and gave me days and times when it was best to call.

When the day came to make the call, there was no answer. I left a message and continued with my routine of the evening. The next evening, I called again and no answer. I left another message. A few minutes later my phone rang, and it was JoAnne. Her voice was so soothing and mellow. We talked for a while, and it was great to reconnect. We covered some of the ground about our

## Trust the Timing

pasts and what we were up to currently. It was exciting to learn more about who she had become. At the end, I asked if she would mind if I called again. She said it would be okay.

After the call, I was thankful to be able to speak to her. I hoped we might become good friends at the very least. At this point in my life, I was not interested in a romantic relationship—yet I felt excited beyond compare. The excitement was purposeful. I hoped to find the answer to the question that had tugged at me for years, to finally find out who JoAnne had become and what the years of her life had taught her.

The next week, I called again, and we had a great conversation. I liked the person she had become. She was nice, soft spoken, and smart. I wanted to get to know her better.

The next time I called I was on duty at the firehouse. It was the last week of June, and I knew my next weekend off was in the middle of July. It had been a long time since I'd asked someone out on a date. I tried to sound casual.

"What are you doing the evening of July 15?"

She said she had planned to visit her son in the mountains that weekend, but the trip had been postponed. Then she asked me why I wanted to know.

"I have some time off that weekend. How would you feel about me taking you out to dinner that Friday night?"

Silence. I thought I might have made her mad. After a few seconds, I asked if she was still on the phone.

"You're going to come all the way down here to Wilmington, North Carolina, just to have dinner with me?"

"Yep, with one catch," I said.

More silence. *Oh boy, she probably thinks I'm a weirdo.*

"What's the catch?" she asked.

"I would like to encumber your day Saturday. To sit and talk about the past to find out what has brought you to this place right now. I don't care if we sit in the backyard sipping on lemonade."

She said yes!

The following evening, I spoke with my friend Jen, who had become like a sister to me.

"Guess what?"

"What?"

"I'm going on a date with a girl."

"Really?"

"Yeah. I gotta travel a little bit."

"Oh? Where're you headed?"

"North Carolina."

Jen raised her eyebrows. I told her about JoAnne, and I guess my excitement was evident. I couldn't stop smiling.

"Good for you!" she said. "But you're awfully excited. Stay grounded."

"I am," I replied, grinning.

## Trust the Timing

JoAnne and I talked on Wednesday evenings in addition to staying connected through emails and Facebook. Anticipating our phone call provided a light of hope for the week. We talked about all kinds of things, but for some reason, I wasn't ready to tell her about Catherine. My friend, who didn't talk about death, had died peacefully just a few days after I found JoAnne. I didn't talk about Catherine much to anyone. That relationship felt so personal. Maybe someday I'd be able to tell JoAnne about Catherine.

It was an exciting couple of weeks getting ready to head south. I lined up care for the dogs; booked a room at the hotel where Caroline, Terry, and Sally had stayed a year earlier; and looked for deals on a rental car. I decided to drive down instead of fly to allow more flexibility—just in case we didn't connect well enough to continue beyond the first date. We'd talked about spending time together Saturday and maybe going to church on Sunday, but you never know how things are going to work in person. JoAnne had commented that I didn't have any pictures of myself on Facebook. (I've never liked having my picture taken.) So I'm sure she wondered what I looked like in real life.

As I prepared for the trip, I also had to make sure I didn't blow a gasket at work.

The atmosphere and the stress from all the administrative changes over the past couple of years were starting to suck the life out of me. I no longer wanted to be there, and the rumor network indicated there would be a reduction of personnel toward the end of the year. I wondered, *Could this be it? Would I be let go and retire at year's end? Interesting possibility.*

I felt pumped up as JoAnne and I planned our date for Friday evening. We had spoken several more times on the phone, and we were both getting excited and nervous at the same time. The week before the trip was challenging as the stress at work neared the boiling point. I knew I was burned out and needed some time off. I had planned to leave work on Thursday at noon but decided to leave earlier. The chief agreed to cover the rest of my shift. He knew what I was going through and about my date seven hundred miles away.

"Good for you," he said. "Have fun."

My plan was to bed down in Virginia and finish the trip Friday morning. That way, I would be fresher than if I'd been driving for twelve hours. Good decision.

I left Connecticut at 4:30 p.m. Rush hour traffic was heavy in the northeast cities, but it didn't matter. I was on a mission! When the traffic eased up, the drive became uneventful, and I talked with JoAnne, off and on, while passing through New Jersey, Delaware, and Maryland. She was concerned I might be tired, so she talked and sang to me until north of Baltimore when we said goodnight. Just south of DC at almost midnight, I witnessed a motor vehicle accident in the lane next to me. A Harley

## Trust the Timing

accelerated off the entrance ramp and suddenly welded itself to the back of a minivan. I couldn't stop safely with all the traffic, so I called it in to emergency services. Now the adrenaline was pumping. Part of me wanted to keep going, but wisdom prevailed, and I finally bunked down around 1:30 a.m.

The next morning, at 8:00 a.m., I started down the road. The timing looked good. Just into North Carolina, I came upon a two-car accident and stopped to assist. I called it in and assessed the seven patients. There were more people than my resources available, so I assigned other people who stopped to help. Fortunately, no one was seriously injured, and I got under way again after turning the scene over to the fire department twelve minutes later. I thought this would put me behind but saw I was still good on time.

We'd estimated me arriving at JoAnne's house at 2:00 p.m. I checked in with her when I stopped for fast food about an hour north of Wilmington. She'd gone to work for a couple of hours that morning and was on her way to pick up groceries. I could hear the excitement in her voice.

Driving into Wilmington a couple of minutes past two in the afternoon, I felt nervous, excited, hopeful, and apprehensive all at the same time. What would I say when I saw her? *Ok, deep breath. Relax!*

I approached the yellow, cottage-like house and knocked on the strong wooden door. Out came JoAnne.

## A Memoir of Finding Love Again

She was beautiful! Flooding through my memory were the thoughts of thirty-nine years prior. A warm embrace and smiles after all these years! We covered some small talk of the trip, and I met Miss Ayla. Then it was off to check in at the hotel. I would pick JoAnne up at five o'clock for our date!

That evening we went out to dinner. I knew nothing of the city, and JoAnne was a most gracious guide. She had chosen a quiet, rustic downtown restaurant near the river where we got reacquainted in person. I was nervous and excited, but I knew I didn't have anything to lose. I had an escape clause because I was only there to find out who she'd become. If we didn't hit it off, I could leave any time. But as we talked, I discovered that not only was she beautiful but I also enjoyed her company. After dinner, we put the leftover appetizer nachos in the car and headed toward the river. I offered my arm as a gentlemanly escort. JoAnne accepted without hesitation.

The boardwalk along the river was crowded, so JoAnne suggested we head upriver away from the activity. We talked about the years past and the experiences that had brought us to this place—with still no questions off the table. What great conversation! And I was with JoAnne after all these years. At one point, I leaned over and gave her a kiss, and she didn't slap me. As we gazed across the river at the amber sunset, I shared with JoAnne my ritual of giving thanks at the end of the day. Then we turned around to the east and saw a bright, full moonrise. *Perfect!*

# Trust the Timing

I had the feeling that this was more than special. In the hours we spent together, JoAnne and I started to connect on an entirely different level. While I was still nervous as a cat on a hot tin roof and surprised I could carry on a conversation without stuttering too much, I also felt moments of peace and serenity because I realized I didn't have to impress her. I could be myself.

We spent most of the next day together and ended up on the south end of Wrightsville Beach. It had been many years since my bare feet had touched sand and saltwater. It felt strange but refreshing. As we relaxed on a blanket, listening to the ocean, JoAnne sang a song to me. It was a Celtic lullaby. Her voice was sweet and soothing. I couldn't remember anyone ever singing to me like that before. A bit later, we walked around to the waterway to catch the golden sunset and another moonrise over our shoulders. As we talked, our conversations transitioned from the intriguing parallels in our pasts to where we were at that moment.

As I drove JoAnne home, I realized how much I liked who she'd become. We were stopped at a traffic light, and I looked over at her. "I don't want this to be a one-date deal. Thirty-nine years ago, when we parted ways, it was not our choice. We have a choice now. Would you like to try to make this work?"

She hesitated for only a second. "Yes," she replied. "One step at a time."

I was on cloud nine! I left that evening with a new

perspective of the future. I didn't know what it would become, but I liked where I was.

My mom had been watching Beep and Oreo. Doodle was in the doggie hotel. I called to check on the dogs, and of course my mother asked about the trip so far.

"Ma, she's beautiful!" I said. My head was spinning. There was new hope and promise in my life. It felt good. One step at a time. Enjoy the journey! So many thoughts! Sleep was going to be a challenge.

The next morning, I opened the car door and still smelled the nachos that had spent Friday night in the back seat. When I went to start the car, nothing happened. It turns out that in my excitement I'd left the lights on Saturday night. The battery was as dead as it could be. I called JoAnne, and she rescued me. We shared a laugh, and off to church we went.

The congregation of Good Shepherd Church welcomed me openly. JoAnne had been attending this church for many years, and she referred to everyone there as her church family. At one point during a hymn, she reached around my elbow to rest her hand on my arm. It felt completely natural. This small bit of affection was another of the many new feelings I experienced that weekend in July.

The visit was coming to an end. I had commitments for the next day, and it was time to say our farewells. We stood in JoAnne's front yard, and I looked in her eyes.

"We went thirty-nine years without seeing each

other," I said. "I don't want to go another thirty-nine days."

JoAnne smiled. "Oh, I have a feeling it won't be that long."

Our embrace hinted at the growing desire to remain together. It was difficult to drive away. I'd had an incredible weekend. Something special had happened.

## 23

## *JoAnne*
# Cloud Nine
(July 2011)

I felt giddy as the time approached for David to arrive and kept telling myself to keep my feet on the ground and to *breathe*. When I saw the tall, handsome man who was my first love standing there at my door, it was almost like a dream, but my pounding heart told me I was wide awake. There was this little peck of a kiss that felt perfectly normal and a friendly embrace.

David came inside to meet Ayla and the dogs. Then we sat on the couch and talked for a bit about his drive down. I began to relax a little as I observed David. His hair was much shorter, neatly trimmed and gleaming with silver highlights. He wasn't as lean as the teenager of my memories. In fact, he had filled out quite nicely. His eyes were still attentive and caring. No matter how firmly my brain told me to be cool and calm, my heart knew something important was going on.

We ate dinner at Paddy's Hollow downtown, which I chose for the relaxed and cozy feeling of the brick walls

# Trust the Timing

and private booths with dark wood, not to mention its proximity to the river. David and I studied each other across the table as we talked. He appeared confident yet thoughtful. He reassured me that there were still no questions off the table. We had talked about our past marriages and relationship challenges on the phone, gradually revealing more details. During dinner, I asked a few more questions, probably some I'd already asked, and he answered patiently. As he shared about his work as a firefighter and EMT and about the things he cared about, I began to recognize that David had become a man of integrity.

After dinner, we walked along the riverfront as a gentle breeze softened the midsummer evening. The weather had been oppressively hot up until this weekend. It was as if David had brought the fresh cooling breezes with him. As the sun started to sink toward the horizon, we sat down on a bench to watch the gold and orange highlights melt together. I took a moment to breathe in the scent of jasmine growing on the iron fence nearby before continuing the interview process.

"What did you learn from your other relationships?" I asked.

"I've learned about the importance of frank, open, and honest communication above all else," he responded with certainty.

That sounded good. Honest communication was definitely a key ingredient.

"What about you? What have you learned?" he asked.

"Many things," I said. "Honest communication is important. Honesty with respect and compassion. And making time for the relationship. Not letting too many other things get in the way of quality time together."

He nodded his understanding.

After a while, I felt relaxed enough to lean back against him. His arms felt strong and comforting as he held me gently. His warm kiss awakened feelings my body had all but forgotten. David was strong, intelligent, considerate, and a perfect gentleman. The euphoria almost overwhelmed me. It felt like a mild but lingering hot flash that went all the way down to my toes. I was thankful for the cool breeze of nightfall.

The next day we went for a walk around Greenfield Lake. David started out at a fast pace, like he had to get to a meeting or something. I pulled his hand gently and asked him to slow down a bit. He smiled knowingly, and we strolled leisurely along the path that curved around the cypress trees, pines, and azalea bushes. I had decided to wear sandals that were more feminine than sneakers—a minor mistake as my feet got a little sore, but I hardly noticed with the gorgeous day. The sky was Carolina blue with a few of those white, puffy clouds, and the temperature was comfortable in the mid-eighties, about ten degrees cooler than the week before.

After the lake, we went back to the house and rested on the couch. I leaned against David quietly,

## Trust the Timing

just breathing and trying to relax. The anticipation and excitement of the past few days had been such a natural high that I felt tired and energized at the same time. I would have liked to have dozed off for a moment, but my senses were too aroused. All I could do was feel David's heartbeat and become slightly intoxicated by the faint, almost subliminal scent of his skin that must have been imprinted on my memory all those years ago.

Late in the afternoon, we went to the south end of Wrightsville Beach for another walk. We took off our shoes to stroll through the cooling sand as we passed people fishing and children playing in the water. We relaxed for a while on a blanket near the ocean, breathing in her freshness and listening to her waves as our fingers played in the sand and touched gently. Then a soft orange glow beckoned us to walk around to the west. I stood in front of David with my back against his chest. He held me gently with his perfectly muscled arms as we watched the sun set across the waterway and gave thanks for the day and our time together. Sunsets can surprise you. When you watch the whole show from beginning to end, there are constant changes. Even after the sun has gone below the horizon and you think it's over, the sunlight can reflect colors of pink and orange off the clouds for a dazzling finish.

After the last colors of sunset faded, we went for pizza and made small talk. Then, on the way home, we talked about the future. David said he didn't want this to be a one-date deal. "Thirty-nine years ago, we had no choice when we parted ways," he said. "We have a choice now. Do you want to try to make this work?"

I took a deep breath. The past two days had been like a dream. But my brain was still telling me to be cautious. I replied firmly, "Yes. But we need to take it one step at a time."

David continued to be respectful and a perfect gentleman. I had mixed feelings about that as my body was experiencing sensations and desires that were waking up hungry after five years in hibernation. It's one thing to give physical pleasure to yourself now and then to make sure things are still working and to release a bit of tension. It's a much different thing to be in the arms of a strong, attractive man who treats you with respectful tenderness.

When he took me back to my house, I was surprised that he didn't even bring up the possibility of going back to his hotel room. I hadn't entirely made up my mind as to how I would respond, though my plan was to say no. But I thought he'd at least mention it.

"I thought you might want to take me back to your hotel room," I admitted.

"Oh, don't think I don't want to," he assured me. "I'd like nothing more than to take your clothes off of you and make mad, passionate love to you."

Then, after a pause, he added, "when the time is right."

We were wise to wait, to take it one step at a time.

# Trust the Timing

The next morning, as I was getting ready for David to come pick me up for church, he called me on the phone.

"Do you have any jumper cables?" He had left the rental car's lights on overnight, and the battery was dead.

I felt flattered that he had forgotten to turn the lights off because I could tell he was the kind of person who was usually careful about such things; he must have been thinking about me pretty hard. I picked him up and took him to buy jumper cables, which he gave me as a present since I didn't have any. After he got the rental car started, we dropped my Jeep off at the house and headed for church.

Introducing David to my Good Shepherd family was fun. I felt a sense of healthy pride in bringing such a handsome and considerate man to church with me. A couple of the older ladies whispered to me, "He's nice looking!" The sparkle in their eyes was likely a reflection of what they saw in mine.

After church, we went back to my house and ate pasta salad that Ayla made with olives, shrimp, and artichoke hearts. It was hard to say goodbye. But this time, we knew it would not be for forty years. As David drove home, we talked on the phone when the traffic was light. As he watched the sun set just before the Washington beltway, I watched the sun set from my backyard and gave thanks for an amazing weekend.

## 24

*David*

# Home and Back Again
(July–October 2011)

When I returned from my first trip to North Carolina, the friends who knew of my journey asked how my weekend went. The smile told it all. I was in a different place. Priorities were shifting. I was focused and determined. Through it all, I also knew I needed to stay grounded.

Over the next couple of weeks, the phone calls became more frequent, and JoAnne and I talked on the phone every night. The conversations grew deeper as we felt more comfortable with each other, at least on the phone.

I knew my next weekend days off started on the twelfth of August. I asked if it was okay to come back down that weekend, and she said yes, again! Flight time was just over four hours compared to the twelve or thirteen driving, and it turned out to be less expensive.

The day arrived for the trip. Up at 3:00 a.m., out the door at 4:00 a.m., airport at 5:00 a.m., boarding at 5:45

a.m. and off we went. The initial flight was uneventful with one hour to the connecting flight. I sent JoAnne text messages on my progress. She had to work that morning and planned to get to the airport about an hour after I landed. Then we would enjoy the weekend together once again. I boarded the plane for the second leg and was waiting for departure when the power failed on the plane. We sat in the dark for six or seven minutes. When the lights came on, a flight attendant announced there had been a mechanical malfunction. We de-planed to wait back in the terminal. At least we were safe.

The flight was delayed for over an hour. New airplane, and off we went. I felt excitement during the climb out. I was on my way again to see JoAnne! When the pilot backed off the power to begin the descent a short time later, I really got excited. Okay, let's get this thing on the ground!

The delay allowed JoAnne to be waiting for me at the airport. I sent her a text message as soon as the airplane hit the ground. I was beside myself as we taxied to the gate. As I hurried down the walkway toward baggage claim, I caught a glimpse of JoAnne. She was radiant. WOW! I knew this weekend was going to be special.

JoAnne had arranged for me to stay at the vacant house belonging to one of her friends, a comfortable place just outside the city. As we talked quietly over lunch, I noticed that JoAnne had started to tear up a bit.

"I'm sorry for getting emotional," she said. "I'm just so happy you're here."

## A Memoir of Finding Love Again

"It's okay. Let it go." I reached for her hand. Then I got up to give her a hug. It felt good that she cared so much. And I understood how she felt.

When we had finished lunch, we moved to the couch. I took out my phone to address some questions she had emailed me about. I knew these questions were important to her. It was a vote of confidence in me that she cared enough to ask important questions and trusted me to tell her the truth. I told her everything she wanted to know. I wanted her to feel special and to know how important she was to me.

After a while, JoAnne got very quiet, so I asked her what she was thinking.

"I think . . . I'm falling in love with you," she said.

"Good," I replied. "So it's okay if I tell you I love you. And I'm going to tell you at least 10,000 more times."

I had loved her since I was fifteen years old.

In a couple of months, I'd gone from not wanting to be in another relationship to wanting nothing more than to be with JoAnne. I knew we needed to take it slow, nice and easy, and one step at a time, but I also knew I was ready to build this relationship.

Later, we went out to dinner downtown. It was the first time I'd worn shorts outside of a gym in about thirty-five years, but it was hot, so I pushed beyond my comfort zone and bared my white legs to Wilmington. After dinner, we caught a little of the sunset at the river. Then we drove to the beach.

## Trust the Timing

We walked along the shore until we found a place for our blanket. For a while, we sat quietly and admired the stunning beauty of silvery moonlight reflecting on the ocean. As we kissed and snuggled on the blanket, things became more passionate. We felt like teenagers again, amazed by the rekindling of the almost-forgotten fire. But we still weren't quite ready to go further. JoAnne pushed me away playfully and jumped up to dance around the blanket while laughing and singing about the moon. I had told her I was allergic to fun, but I was beginning to think there was another way to be. There was hope for me.

On Sunday, we went to church, and then it was the hard part: time to go to the airport. Before I went through security, we held each other for a moment. Then we kissed goodbye. As much as I loved flying, climbing out was emotionally difficult. It felt like I was leaving a part of me behind.

Major changes at work were imminent. Though I would be eligible for retirement at year's end, and looked forward to that option, I let the powers that be know that I planned to stay on into the next year. This way, I could be in the best financial order possible. I planned to utilize my vacation time and days off to travel south and to pay for it with overtime.

Unfortunately, scheduled overtime and business commitments made earlier in the year kept me from traveling to North Carolina on my next long break. I would have to wait five weeks to see JoAnne again. It felt like an eternity!

Somehow we managed with phone calls and emails until our September visit. For this visit, we decided to invite some of JoAnne's friends over to the house where I was staying. We made vegetarian chili and discovered how much we enjoyed cooking together. I didn't mind supporting JoAnne in her efforts to abstain from meat and was pleased to find out that she shared my love of garlic. It was fun preparing a meal for her friends. In addition to Carla who owned the house with her husband, I met JoAnne's friend Barbara, and Marci and Paul who brought over a karaoke machine. I was slowly learning to relax a bit and getting comfortable, not enough to sing karaoke but enough to enjoy JoAnne singing "Here Comes the Rain Again," sounding like Annie Lennox.

When it was time to go back north, leaving was hard, but I knew we would see each other a lot more in the month ahead. JoAnne and I saw each other every two weeks through the month of October. I was fortunate to have the flexibility of schedule and vacation time to travel more that month, and JoAnne flew up for a weekend. I introduced her to some close friends and family and reintroduced her to Mom. Over the past few months, when we talked about JoAnne, Mom would ask me, "Are you happy?"

"Yes, I am," I'd tell her.

## Trust the Timing

"I like seeing you happy," she'd say with a warm smile.

The dogs liked JoAnne right off the bat, which was a relief since Beep had been known to be aggressive with strangers. Beep could tell JoAnne was a dog person and clearly not a stranger.

The fast-paced weekend was all too short. Once again, when we parted at the airport, it was not pleasant to watch JoAnne enter the security line by herself. There was a growing part of me that said, *I should be with her, by her side.*

## 25

### JoAnne

# It's Never Too Late
(July–October 2011)

The euphoria of David's first visit lingered for weeks as I floated around on that natural high yet still hearing the faraway voice of caution as it called out: *Hey, what happened to keeping your feet on the ground?* I'd learned the hard way that people are on their best behavior in the beginning of a relationship. One of my coworkers who enjoyed doing background checks when she had trouble sleeping offered to investigate David for me. This was something I promised myself I'd do up front after the last two relationships.

Curious about how he would respond, I told David about the promise I'd made to myself and that I was having him investigated.

"Do you want my social security number?" he asked.

"Are you serious?" I wondered if he was being sarcastic.

"Yes, I'm serious," he replied. "I know how important it is when you make a promise to yourself. I'm going to help you keep that promise."

## Trust the Timing

My investigator confirmed public record details about David and couldn't find any record of criminal activity. She reported that he was in the Rotary Club and that this was a plus because they did a lot of service work in the community. She also noted that he sent flowers to me at work. Her report concluded with, "Go for Launch." My fears eased a bit.

David and I got into the habit of talking on the phone almost every night at nine o'clock. I would make sure I had my shower and was ready for his call, and when the phone rang, my heart started dancing. It felt like being in high school again. We talked for at least an hour, some nights for two or three hours, and continued to ask each other lots of questions. Since no questions were off the table, I asked away.

I asked about his past relationships, his spiritual beliefs, and money issues. I gave him any details about myself he asked for. We didn't want there to be any big surprises. I found a fun book with 459 "Intimate Questions" on a wide variety of topics, which came in handy for those times when we didn't know what else to say but didn't want to hang up the phone. But silence was okay too.

One of my favorite questions from David was, "What would you do if you knew you could not fail and money were no object?" I loved that he was interested in my hopes and dreams.

"I'd have a place in nature," I began, opening my

imagination. "A small farm, maybe. Where people could come to relax, and meditate, and get healthy. We'd have art therapy, and music therapy, and yoga. Sort of a spiritual retreat center. And I'd have an art studio. And comfy places to write. And a fire pit, and . . ." Doubt wanted to creep back in. "If money were no object," I reminded myself, "I could have an animal sanctuary. For dogs mainly, but who knows?"

David allowed some silence, letting me revel in my dreams until I came back to the conversation.

"Thank you for asking that. No one's ever asked me a question like that before."

"It feels good, doesn't it?"

"Yes, it does. What would you do, if you could do anything you wanted?"

"I'd fly. I'd have my own plane, so I could fly whenever I wanted."

"I get motion sickness at the drop of a hat. And I should also tell you that I'm afraid of heights. But if I have Dramamine, I'd fly anyway, for the view. I bet the view would be worth it."

"Oh, the views are amazing!" David went on to describe sights he'd seen flying over the New England coastline and over snow-covered landscapes on moonlit nights. It sounded dreamy and exciting.

"I'd like to fly with you sometime," I told him.

I was falling fast for this man. I needed to grab hold of something and lay some things out on the table. There were a couple of things I put in an email when my head was clear. I expressed concern about him having a high energy level and wanted him to know that my energy level fluctuated a lot. Then I wrote, "So, what are you looking for in this relationship?"

David responded that he wanted to talk about these things face-to-face when he flew down in August.

On the morning of his arrival, I had a therapy group to do at work. David, being gracious as well as an "airplane nerd," agreed to wait an hour or so at the airport for me to pick him up. It turned out his flight was delayed, so when I got there, he was still in the air. I got to wait for him. This time, I was much more excited than nervous. I had about fifteen minutes to wait but could not stay still, even with my breathing techniques. There was all this energy in my body, and it was too much to contain.

In later weeks, it would be just plain fun to wait at the airport. Being there a little early and watching people greet loved ones with hugs would add to my own joy. One time there was a little girl waiting with her mom. She looked about three years old. When I ran to hug and kiss David, the little girl must have thought her person had arrived. I felt her hugging my legs from behind. Her mom apologized needlessly. It was so funny and touching that this little girl got caught up in our excitement. She was ready to hug somebody! I thought, *There should be an airport greeter to welcome people who don't have someone there to meet them.*

But this first time I waited for David at the airport, the excitement was almost too intense. My heart beat as fast and as hard as if I was running a mile, but I could only pace. For the first time in my life, I *had* to pace back and forth, and I could not stop grinning. I wondered if people thought I was crazy, but it didn't matter. I kept watching for him to come down the ramp. As each tall man started to come around the corner, my excitement rose, then dropped slightly when I saw it wasn't him. Finally, it was him! He was smiling and walking toward me. It felt like one of those old TV commercials where the man and the woman are running toward each other in slow motion. With David's embrace, our energy collided like two powerful waves flowing into each other. Even though my mind kept trying to tell me to keep my feet on the ground and be careful, my body, my heart, already knew.

I'd arranged for David to stay at the vacant house of a gracious friend. I didn't want him to have to stay at a hotel, but we weren't ready for him to stay at my two-bedroom house. From the airport, we picked up a couple of sandwiches and took them to the house just outside of town. Trees and hedges bordered the property, and a large, natural backyard gave a rural feel to the place. Simple furnishings with walls of harvest gold and sage provided a comfortable setting for us to focus on just the two of us.

After lunch, we made our way to the couch in the living room. David took each of my questions and concerns seriously as he responded to my email. He reassured me that the energy difference was not a big thing. He was aware that his energy could be intense. "When you want to rest, you rest," he said. "We are not in a competition."

"What do you want from this relationship?" I asked. I wanted to find out without too many clues from me.

"I want a long-term, kind, loving, and gentle relationship, a relationship that is based on communication and respect."

*He's saying the right words,* I thought. *But it feels right, too.*

We talked about integrity and honesty, and I decided to tell him some secrets. I'd read that you shouldn't do that early in a relationship, but I had to see his reaction before I got in too deep. I started with some of the challenges I'd had with my kids.

Those secrets didn't seem like a big deal to him.

"Okay. So, what makes your kids different from so many other kids?"

"Well, because my kids aren't supposed to have those kinds of problems. I thought things would be so different."

"We all have our challenges as parents and as kids," he reassured.

I took a chance and told him some things that I only tell people who I trust not to judge me. I knew that secrets brought into the light often dry up and crumble into dust. But it depends on who you're telling. Compared to many of the secrets I'd heard, mine weren't all that bad. There were no bodies buried in my backyard. But for me, they were embarrassing secrets because they were mine.

David listened carefully and did not judge. He accepted. His words told me he was open-minded and, more importantly, caring rather than critical.

He put his arms around me and encouraged me to lean back against him as we sat on the couch. I felt the muscles in his chest. I felt his heartbeat. His fingers caressed my hair as his scent caressed my brain. I could have gone to sleep, but my heart wouldn't slow down enough.

"I feel like you're treating me like a princess," I told him.

"No, I'm not," he said. "I'm treating you like a queen."

"You better watch out. I could get used to this, and then I'll expect to be treated like a queen."

"Good. Get used to it," he replied.

I relaxed, letting that soak in. *Get used to it.*

"So, what are you thinking?" he asked after a while.

I took a deep breath. Did I dare say what I was thinking? *I can't be the one to say it first.* But the words spilled out of my mouth on their own.

"I think . . . I'm falling in love with you."

"Good. Then it's okay if I say it." His lips moved close to my ear. "I love you."

I sat up and turned to look at his blue eyes. David

smiled. Then he kissed me even better than before.

We realized we had never stopped loving each other. Yes, our love had faded and become buried under forty years of separate lives seven hundred miles apart. But it had never completely died. It had been there all the time, waiting quietly.

When I took David to the airport, just before he went through security, he held up his hand in front of me with his two middle fingers down and his index and pinky fingers up.

"Do you know what this means?" he asked.

"No. But I've always wanted to learn sign language," I told him.

"It means I love you."

I made the sign, touching my index and pinky fingers to his, and said, "I love you, David." Hearing myself say those words reminded me of the significance of what was happening and who it was happening with. Who would have imagined that, at the age of fifty-five, I would be standing in an airport saying "I love you" to my first love?

I watched him clear security and then start toward the corridor. He turned and gave me the "I love you" sign again. I held up my hand to return the sign. Then he was gone.

I walked outside missing him and remembered the time he left me when I was sixteen. But I knew this time was different. This time, he would be back.

David returned to Wilmington in September. When we

hugged, my nose nuzzled his neck. I couldn't get over the smell of him. It wasn't any cologne, aftershave, or deodorant. It was the mild, almost-imperceptible smell of his skin. My nose wanted to consume his scent. Was it just a matter of compatible pheromones? Or was the memory of David's natural scent imprinted on my sixteen-year-old brain from all that serious kissing with my first love? Maybe it was both. But, either way, I heard somewhere that liking someone's natural smell was a good sign.

Though my brain remembered David well, my father didn't. Dad must have been working a lot in those days not to remember my first boyfriend. When I told Dad about David over the phone, Dad wanted to know if he had been married before and wasn't happy to know David had been divorced twice. Dad was being protective. He didn't want me to be hurt again. When they first met, Dad was quieter than usual, listening carefully, studying. After a couple of months, Dad started to come around.

"Well, at least he doesn't have long hair," he conceded.

In October, I flew to Connecticut to visit David for the weekend. Ayla, who was going to the community college, stayed home with Jesse and Mary. It had been many years since I'd flown on a plane or even been out of North Carolina, so the trip was my own little adventure, just like I'd imagined in the beginning of the year when I made myself stop looking for a man until Ayla graduated.

## Trust the Timing

Now, I was flying to Connecticut to see my first love.

David's mother was still as lovely and as kind as ever. As a teenager, I'd felt so comfortable with her that I wasn't embarrassed when she yelled at us to keep the bedroom door open. I remembered David's mother and I sitting in her car waiting for David and his brother at the motorcycle track. She had let me put eyeshadow on her eyelids, and I thought it strange that her eyelids were wrinkled because she didn't seem old at all. Now I had wrinkled eyelids, too.

I got to meet several of David's friends and other family members. It was funny to hear David being called "Grampa Dave." I hadn't been called Grandma yet, but that was coming soon.

And, of course, I got to meet The Three Amigos—Beep, Oreo, and Doodle—whom I'd heard so much about. Beep was only a little jealous and more curious about this new person who wasn't just dropping by. She whined about not having her snuggle buddy all to herself, especially when David removed the steps she used to get up on the high bed. We put a blanket down for her in the other bedroom, and she eventually accepted that there was a new alpha female in the house, at least for the weekend.

We needed time and space to become comfortable with each other. We had discovered that rushing spontaneously into midlife sex after years of celibacy didn't work well for us. We had to take a few steps back.

# A Memoir of Finding Love Again

Snuggling and cuddling were simply divine. We took our time exploring the pleasures of long, soft kisses and intoxicating caresses that would, in time, turn into full-blown passion, making us feel like we were in our twenties again.

Over the weekend, David showed me the cozy New England towns where he grew up. The charming town of Mystic, with its old shops and waterfront, reminded me of Wilmington, and Mystic Pizza really did taste like "a slice of heaven," though being with David might have had something to do with it.

On Sunday, we drove to David's church. Being such a flatlander, the winding, wooded roads reminded me of the mountains of North Carolina, especially since autumn had already brought cooler temperatures to Connecticut. The little white church sat on a hill overlooking the countryside. Pastor Dave and the congregation welcomed me warmly, easing my fear of Baptists that had originated with the abduction nightmares of my rebellious youth. Pastor Dave wasn't scary at all. The thoughtful twinkle in his eyes hinted at the wealth of wisdom and kindness in his heart.

After church, we went back to the house for lunch. Then it was time to get ready to leave. David took me to the airport and, after our goodbye kiss, gave the "I love you" sign. On the flight home, I sang a song in my head. It was the old Eagles song "Desperado." I'd been singing it to myself, changing the words a little. Allowing myself

## Trust the Timing

to fall in love again felt a little like jumping off a cliff and not knowing for sure what waited below. But the fears that teased me could get in the way of real happiness. David was the best thing that had happened to me in a long time. I decided to open my heart and give love one more chance.

## 26

*David*

# Birthday Weekend
(October–December 2011)

The notice came in late October that my position at the factory was being eliminated. My last day would be in mid-November. I was being forced to retire right after my fifty-fifth birthday. At least there would be a severance package, compensation for my investment of thirty-five years. I felt like I was being cast aside, but I also felt relieved. I knew it was time to move on and pass the torch to the younger guys. The timing was perfect. JoAnne and I had been planning my holiday travel; now, we could have more time together.

Even so, scheduling conflicts and previous commitments kept us apart for three weeks. It felt like three months! I had come to enjoy seeing JoAnne every two weeks and wanted to see her more. Finally, Thanksgiving week opened a window of opportunity. During this visit, we spent ten incredible days together. I stayed at JoAnne's house, and we grew closer and more comfortable with each other as I realized, *This is really*

## Trust the Timing

*where I need to be.* There were no doubts.

Taking Jesse and Mary for an evening walk, the air felt cool and crisp but nowhere near as cold as Connecticut. I noticed a vacant house on the corner and recalled all the times I'd thought about moving south. Now there was a better reason than the weather.

"What do you think about me moving to North Carolina?" I asked.

"I think that's an interesting idea," she said, rolling it around. "I like that idea."

We didn't make any definite plans about me relocating; we just let the idea germinate.

Driving away from her house on the Monday after Thanksgiving brought a horrible feeling of emptiness.

On my arrival back to Connecticut, it was time to start getting ready for a move. There was a lot of stuff I needed to get organized and get rid of. But there was something else I needed to do, too. JoAnne's birthday weekend was fast approaching, and I wanted to make something special for her. So, for the first time in four years, I headed down to the basement workshop. It took the better part of the day to get the tools back in shape. Waking up my woodworking skills felt good, like coming home from a long trip. I was making projects from the heart.

I finished the last of the projects with a day to spare. Everything was packed into the suitcase, and off I went for a weekend of birthday celebrations. Each day I planned to give JoAnne another gift.

On December 8, I flew to Wilmington via Charlotte. There I watched in horror as the baggage handler lifted every bag to shoulder height and dropped it onto the conveyor loading into the airplane. *Please let there be no damage to my gifts.*

JoAnne picked me up at the airport. Her eyes sparkled with her radiant smile. We had a little quiet time before her son and his family got there from the other side of the state. When they arrived, it was a reality check of incredible excitement. There were little people in a strange house with two dogs, and they had to explore everything! It was an action-packed evening to say the least and the beginning of a very special weekend.

The next day we had plans to go with JoAnne's church group to Brookgreen Gardens, an outdoor art conservatory in South Carolina.

On December 9, we picked up the rental car and headed to the church for carpooling. A two-hour drive later, we were there. It was a beautiful late-fall afternoon with a festive chill in the air.

While it was still daylight, we broke away from the rest of the group and walked around the gardens, enjoying the magnificent works of sculpture from Greek and Roman mythology. The facility had been a rice plantation in its early years and still had remnant buildings from the

## Trust the Timing

old days. Several giant live oaks hung with Spanish moss lined each side of the main walkway. The conservatory area was impeccably manicured, and the reflecting pools were spectacular. It was a complementary blend of art and nature.

Before dinner, as the sun set behind the marsh grass, JoAnne joined me in giving thanks for all the blessings bestowed on us—finding each other again, being in this place, our time together.

We ate a Calabash seafood dinner in a huge white tent with church family. Then we left the group to stroll back along the walkway between the giant live oaks. Strings of twinkling lights started to come on, and volunteers lit hundreds of luminaries, transforming the gardens into a different place than the one we'd walked through an hour earlier. Musicians played classic holiday melodies and Celtic tunes along the way. The full moon, rising in the east, cast her own silvery light to enhance the mystical feel of the evening.

Up to this point, JoAnne and I had not spoken the "M" word. We had talked of a long-term relationship and our commitments to each other. In our own ways, we had each given thought to marriage, but we had not broached the subject out loud. As we would discuss later, several of our friends had asked us if we were talking about marriage. They could see that we were very much in love and a good fit.

I felt excited yet anxious about proposing. It was a

big deal, and my track record wasn't that great. I knew I wanted to spend the rest of my life with JoAnne, but was I good enough? Had I grown enough? Could she see enough good in me beyond my flaws? Plus, I hadn't gotten her an engagement ring yet!

As we walked through the gardens, we talked about a wide range of subjects and how beautiful everything was. Then we took a path less-traveled, leading toward the back of the gardens where smaller sculptures complemented the softly lit native flora. Going slowly, hand in hand, we could talk with a level of intimacy.

"What do you want your future to look like?" I asked her.

*"I want you to be in my future."* JoAnne smiled. *Did she know what I was thinking?*

"I want you in my future too," I assured her.

Our pace slowed as we made the turn to a quiet area and admired the large white globes suspended on ten-foot poles. They glowed like giant, ethereal lollipops. The moon above smiled at the round spheres attempting to imitate her.

*It's the perfect time to ask her. What if she says yes? Why would you want to pass that up?*

I turned to face JoAnne and looked into her soft green eyes.

"Will you marry me?"

"Yes." She answered without hesitation. Then she grinned. "But you have to get down on one knee."

"Do you want me to ask you again?"

"Yes."

The moment of minor awkwardness was a small price to pay for my queen of hearts.

So I knelt down on one knee. "JoAnne, will you marry me?"

"Yes!" She laughed. "Of course I will!"

We floated through the rest of the evening and talked of our wedding plans, feeling quietly exhilarated. She never asked about a ring, but we would take care of that later. We called Pastor Dave in Connecticut to share the news but decided not to tell anyone else until we spoke to JoAnne's dad the next morning. On the drive home, we had two friends riding with us. It was a challenge, but we didn't say a word about our secret.

The next morning, at nine o'clock, I called JoAnne's dad.

"What's wrong?" he asked. He wasn't used to us calling him so early.

"Nothing's wrong. I just wanted to give you a little bit of news."

"Yeah? What's that?" Now there was a hint of annoyance.

"I've asked JoAnne to marry me, and she agreed. We wanted you to be one of the first to know."

There was only a slight pause.

"Okay. Glad nothing's wrong. I'm getting ready for church."

## A Memoir of Finding Love Again

"Yep. I'll talk to you later," I said. I knew he'd need time to process the news and that he'd come around.

After calling JoAnne's dad, we headed to church where there was a custom of the "Good News Minute." JoAnne patiently waited her turn and reported the previous evening's proposal. There was immediate applause from JoAnne's church family. *Our* church family. Then someone asked, "Did you say yes?"

"Yes!" JoAnne grinned. The joyful excitement set the tone for the remainder of the weekend and our future.

That evening, we put up the Christmas tree. I had not put up a tree for many years. It felt good and right. JoAnne understood the meaning of Christmas. Decorating the tree was done with a lighthearted sense of caring and tradition. I gave her the wooden ornaments I had made years ago. They glowed with a soft luster among the lights. On Monday, I gave her the three tea-light candleholders I had made from old chestnut with purple, amber, and blue stained glass recovered from a window I'd replaced at the house in Connecticut.

Tuesday was JoAnne's birthday. We took Jesse and Mary for a birthday hike at Carolina Beach State Park. The air was crisp as we walked along the marsh trail and through the forest of longleaf pines to a fifty-foot sand dune overlooking the Cape Fear River. Then JoAnne took us off the main trail onto a deer trail. I figured she knew where she was going, but we were lost for a while. She didn't seem worried. Her look of concentration

## Trust the Timing

was regularly interrupted by little smiles as she enjoyed the process of figuring out where we were. Then there was the triumphant grin when we found the main trail leading to the parking lot.

That night, I gave JoAnne the jewelry box I had carefully crafted from light maple and rich cherry. She ran her hand over the smooth wood and smiled. Each of the gifts had miraculously made the journey safely and still in one piece.

There I was, with all those past successes and failures, having picked myself up off the floor on so many occasions, now engaged to be married to the most beautiful, wonderful person I had ever met.

Being in JoAnne's life is a gift I thank God for every day. She was my first love so many years ago, and she is my last love.

There is something to be said about Hope, Trust, Faith, and Belief. Our meeting when we were young was not by chance. The move to North Carolina in 1971 was part of a plan. The move back to Connecticut in 1972 was not a mistake. I needed to unlearn many lessons taught to me. We both needed to go through the trials of life, make mistakes, and learn the lessons we needed to learn to live this amazing life and to be ready to continue learning and growing *together*.

We never know *what* God has in store for us. Believe. Trust. Have Faith. And never give up Hope. Be open to

## A Memoir of Finding Love Again

the possibilities. An amazing life awaits us and is here now when we realize that lessons are offered to prepare us for the wonderful life ahead.

It's ours for the believing.

# Epilogue
## (2012)

W*hy can't I find those pictures?* I remembered looking at them in an old photo album for years. Pictures of other old boyfriends were there in the album. Why were the pictures of David and me missing? I wouldn't have thrown them away, would I? There was no reason to have thrown them away.

It would be so much fun to look at them now. I remembered one in particular that Caroline had taken in her front yard of David and I kissing. I was wearing a poncho with fringe on the bottom. I must have looked at that picture a lot to remember that kind of detail. It would be great to have old pictures of us blown up or framed for our wedding a couple of months away in December. But I'd looked through all the photo albums and couldn't find them anywhere. Where did they go? It didn't make any sense.

I hoped we could at least find David's class picture in my high school yearbook. The 1974 yearbook had been downstairs since the girlfriends visited, but the 1972 yearbook must still be up in the attic, I thought. So David and I climbed up into the attic to look for it. We found the yearbook and David's sullen-looking class picture. He'd written the words "Remember me always" at the top of the picture and "Love, Dave" at the bottom.

"Aw, how sweet," I said. "I did remember you. And I'm so glad you remembered me. I'm so glad you found me again."

"I'm glad I found you again too," David said, leaning over to kiss me.

Then I noticed a white square box near where the yearbook had been. I opened it up and recognized the banner of green cloth on which one of my friends, Debbie somebody, had batiked the letters DAVID in red as a gift. I remembered it being tacked up on my bedroom wall in tenth grade. I lifted the banner to unfold it and glanced back down into the box. *And there they were!*

"I found them!"

"What did you find?"

"The pictures of us! I found them! They're right here in this box!"

There were several photos. Most of them were of David and I kissing at my parents' house. Mom must have taken those. Then I saw the dramatic black-and-white photo of us kissing at Caroline's house. The photo was smaller than the one I remembered, but I could see I had on the fringed poncho. David's hair was longer and fuller than I remembered. The picture was so romantic, so full of passion. Our eyes were closed, and our lips were almost touching in that moment they like to draw out in old movies.

## Trust the Timing

"Why did I put them up here?" I wondered. *Why did I take only the photos with David out of the photo album and put them up here in the attic?* I conjured up a vague memory of taking them out of the album years ago but had no idea why, except maybe the feeling that they were from another lifetime. Had I felt these pictures were different and should be kept safe in a special place and on a higher level, perhaps? Who knows? I had found them again when the time was right. That's what mattered. They would be perfect for our table of memories at the wedding reception.

Terry, Sally, and Caroline came to Wilmington two days before the wedding. I picked up my wedding dress and took it to their hotel room because with all of David's stuff now in my house—*our house!*—there wasn't room to hide such a big dress.

Fitting David's stuff in our two-bedroom bungalow had taken considerable purging, organizing, and arranging, but it was worth it. The garage out back overflowed with workbenches, tools, saws, clamps, and all sorts of guy stuff. David brought six truckloads down from Connecticut in February and March. Doodle loved riding shotgun, so she wouldn't have to go to the doggie hotel and could get acquainted with Mary and Jesse. Jesse was fine with Doodle, but little Mary had to step down as alpha female. It was not an easy adjustment and would take time. Over the next couple of years, David and I had to learn to step up our roles as pack leaders to prevent problems.

After the last truckload, Doodle and the truck stayed in Wilmington. David flew back to Connecticut and brought Beep and Oreo back in the car that had been given to him by the family of the woman he had taken care of before she died. I had been so moved by that story when he told me about Catherine and comforted by David's capacity to care.

During the twelve-hour drive south, poor Oreo stood up in the front seat, whining, panting, and drooling in spite of the medication that was supposed to sedate him. The only time he sat down was when they stopped at rest areas. As soon as they got to Wilmington, we walked all five dogs as a pack, which went better than we expected. Later, there were skirmishes on the home front between Doodle and Mary or between Doodle and Beep (with Oreo as Beep's backup), but none required trips to the vet. The stepdogs became part of our blended family.

But back to the dress! It was a vintage gown of white chiffon from Camille's, a local resale shop. The lacy, beaded bodice accentuated my figure, and the portrait collar gave me a regal snow-queen look that I decided worked well for December (even though it rarely snows in Wilmington). The sparkly emerald slippers I found after weeks of searching completed the look.

The girlfriends' hotel was on the beach and had an oceanfront balcony. On the day before the wedding,

Terry called me.

"I have some bad news," she said. "We were playing around with the dress on the balcony, and the wind just grabbed it away! I'm so sorry. It's somewhere out in the ocean."

"Oh, you're so funny, Terry," I said.

"No, I'm serious! We're going to have to go find you another dress!"

"I don't believe you."

"I'm telling you the truth! Ask Sally."

"Yep, it's true," Sally said, matter-of-factly. I heard something like muffled snorting in the background.

"So why are you laughing?" I asked.

"I'm not laughing. Who's laughing?"

Terry got back on the phone. "I'm trying not to cry," Terry said, sniffling. "I feel so bad about it. Caroline, *you* tell her what happened."

"Leave me out of this!" Caroline called out. "*I* wasn't the one playing around with the dress on the balcony."

They tried to keep it up, but I didn't believe them. Not really.

After the rehearsal dinner, I went to hang out with my girlfriends in their hotel room. And there was the dress hanging up safe and sound and ready for them to bring it to the church the next day.

"Well, I see the dress is still here." I tried to sound matter-of-fact, not wanting them to think I ever believed their shenanigans. They just snickered.

## A Memoir of Finding Love Again

That night we talked about all the awkward, messy, and wonderful times we'd been through since high school. We talked about our hopes for the future, realizing the solidarity of friendship in spite of the miles and the infrequency of our visits. There's nothing like spending time with old girlfriends who are still there for you after all those years, especially when you get the feeling they always will be.

December 1, 2012: my wedding day. Just over forty-one years had passed since the evening I met David at Terry's garage party. Nerves of joy danced throughout my body as I got ready. Having decided on a small wedding party, Ayla was my maid of honor, and David's son Alex was his best man. My girlfriends and David's mother sat up front. David's aunt and Alex's wife, along with Mary from my church family, were all ready with cameras.

*Inhale . . . Exhale . . .* I reminded myself as I walked from the parish hall to the front door of the church where my dad was waiting. I had put aside my feminist resistance to the tradition of being "given away" so that I could honor my father because he deserved to be honored in as many ways as possible.

"Wow!" Dad whispered when he saw me. He was impressed. Ayla went first in her olive-green and gold medieval gown and her long red-gold hair. Then my dad walked me down the aisle. It was a strange feeling to be simply walking with my heart beating at running speed.

## Trust the Timing

But I wasn't scared. I was *excited* like on the day David came back to me in July and the day I waited for him at the airport. Still, today was different. Today, I was getting married!

*Inhale . . . Exhale . . .*

I felt my mom smiling down on us, her angel eyes twinkling with joy as I approached David. This tall, handsome, wonderful man standing there in a tux (did I mention he is handsome?) was smiling with so much love for *me*. He wants to marry *me!*

We joined hands. And then, under the loving gaze of the Good Shepherd, I married the man of my dreams. My first love. My last love. The love of my life.

*This is for all the lonely people*
*Thinking that life has passed them by*
*Don't give up until you drink from the silver cup*
*And never take you down or never give you up*
*You never know until you try.*[1]

---

1
**LONELY PEOPLE**
Words & Music by DAN PEEK and CATHERINE L. PEEK
Copyright © 1974 (Renewed) WB MUSIC CORP.
All Rights Reserved
Used By Permission of ALFRED MUSIC

# Acknowledgements

First, I thank God and my guardian angels for watching over me, guiding me, loving me, and protecting me through this journey and of course for bringing my soulmate to me when the time was perfect.

I thank David for being open to God's grace and guidance that helped him find me when we were both ready and for his patience in the process of bringing forth difficult memories as I interviewed him for this book.

I thank my dad for teaching me that *nothing is impossible* and my mom for her gentle, loving spirit. I thank my sisters Linda and Mary Kaye, now angels in heaven with Dad and Mom.

I thank David's mother for her loving acceptance of me and for sharing her memories.

Thank you to my children, Ayla and Zack. And thank you to my loyal four-legged companions who were there for me through the hard times. I hope to see you again.

Others I wish to thank for their help in the writing of this book are:

Shawna Kenney, who in her online workshop first opened my eyes to the process of creative writing

Editor Andi Cumbo-Floyd of God's Whisper Farm and her online writing community http://www.andilit.com

Andrea Barilla Editing and Writing Services http://www.andreabarilla.com/, who provided meticulous copy editing and an earlier beta read

Word Weavers of Wilmington, whose members provided both critique and encouragement

ExpertSubjects.com for book cover design, formatting, and interior design

My Beta Readers: Dot, Izzi, Leigh, Jana, Kay, and Andrea

*Salt Magazine*, who published "Perfect Timing," the short version of *Trust the Timing*, in July of 2014

Shawn Smucker at http://shawnsmucker.com/

Thank you to my family at The Church of the Good Shepherd.

Thank you to my girlfriends Terry, Sally, and Caroline. (Caroline took the cover photo, circa 1972.)

And thank you to all my encouraging supporters on Facebook and on WordPress.

(Back cover art by JoAnne Macco)

www.ingramcontent.com/pod-product-compliance
Lightning Source LLC
Chambersburg PA
CBHW060148050426
42446CB00013B/2724